Indigenous and Christian Perspectives in Dialogue

Religion and Borders

Series Editor: Alexander Y. Hwang, Xavier University

Traditional borders and boundaries are challenged, tested, defended, and redefined in unprecedented ways. Our current crises can be seen as a consequence of conflicting interpretations of the meaning and purpose of borders and boundaries—tribal, political, national, theological, religious, social, familial, sexual, gender, and psychological, among others. The crises of immigration, refugees, famine, disease, poverty, wars, misogyny, sexism, and the environment originate from reified misunderstandings of borders and boundaries. Borders and boundaries define who we are and who we are not; they divide those who suffer and perish from those who flourish and survive. Religion, itself based on "holiness," or separateness, plays a vital role—both as object and subject—in better understanding borders and boundaries. *Religion and Borders* interrogates and reconceptualizes the nature and function of borders and the role that religion plays in enforcing or overturning barriers. This series will welcome different scholarly approaches that examine the connection between religion and borders/boundaries, broadly defined. It aims to illuminate how religion—as a sociocultural phenomenon and a discipline—constitutes itself on the premise of borders, while containing within itself the resources, instincts, and practices to resist boundaries and enclosures.

Volumes in the series will not only explore the methodological and theoretical dimensions of the discipline, but will also engage with salient social and political issues, particularly the various crises that are deeply embedded in religious discourse (e.g., migration, environment, public health, sexuality, poverty, war/violence). Projects that engage and draw upon comparative theology, comparative religion, multireligious sources, interreligious engagement, and interdisciplinary perspectives are especially welcome.

Titles in the Series
Indigenous and Christian Perspectives in Dialogue: Kairotic Place and Borders
  by Allen G. Jorgenson

Indigenous and Christian Perspectives in Dialogue

Kairotic Place and Borders

Allen G. Jorgenson

LEXINGTON BOOKS
Lanham • Boulder • New York • London

Published by Lexington Books
An imprint of The Rowman & Littlefield Publishing Group, Inc.
4501 Forbes Boulevard, Suite 200, Lanham, Maryland 20706
www.rowman.com

6 Tinworth Street, London SE11 5AL, United Kingdom

Copyright © 2021 by The Rowman & Littlefield Publishing Group, Inc.

Excerpt from "Sibyl" from *Opened Ground: Selected Poems, 1966–1996*, by Seamus Heaney. Copyright © 1998 by Seamus Heaney. Reprinted by permission of Farrar, Straus and Giroux.

Excerpt from "Out in the Open" from *The Deleted World* by Tomas Tranströmer. Translation copyright © 2006 by Robin Robertson. Reprinted by permission of Farrar, Straus and Giroux.

All rights reserved. No part of this book may be reproduced in any form or by any electronic or mechanical means, including information storage and retrieval systems, without written permission from the publisher, except by a reviewer who may quote passages in a review.

British Library Cataloguing in Publication Information Available

Library of Congress Control Number: 2020949029

ISBN 9781793619679 (cloth) | ISBN 9781793619693 (pbk) ISBN 9781793619686 (epub)

*To my grandparents
Whose sundry border crossings make possible my own.*

Contents

Acknowledgments	ix
Introduction	xi
1 Indigenous Insights	1
2 Luther and Kenotic Space	21
3 Schleiermacher and Harmonic Place	37
4 The Poetic Potency of Place	55
5 Place at the Margins, Hope, and Living Interfaithfully	75
Bibliography	93
Index	101
About the Author	105

Acknowledgments

This volume is dedicated to my grandparents: Zaccaria and Josepha (née Skarpeness) Jorgenson on my father Kenneth's side, and Rudolph and Adelgunda (née Schendel) on my mother Lakadja's (Kay's) side. I never knew my paternal grandmother and have no recollections of my paternal grandfather—as he died when I was still an infant. I have warm memories of my maternal grandparents. But the tales I hear of both sets of grandparents remind me that I am where I am because of their dreams, sacrifices, and perseverance. They all crossed borders, geographical and more, for the sake of their families and we are deeply indebted to them. It seems like such a small thing to acknowledge them in this book, but perhaps this act will prod me to vigilance in taking place seriously and pondering constantly the role of borders in my own life.

Of course, my grandparents, like all settlers across Turtle Island (North America), benefited from land (and other) opportunities that came at horrific costs to the Indigenous peoples of this land. I owe a huge debt to those from these communities who have schooled me in important ways. I think in particular of Archbishop Mark MacDonald, Ray Aldred, Adrian Jacobs, the late Father Norm Casey, the Rev. Rosalyn Elm, the late Leona Moses, the Rev. Canon Virginia "Ginny" Doctor, Elder Jean Becker, Kelly Laurila, Melissa Ireland, Erin Hodson, Elder Banakonda Kennedy-Kish Bell, Trevor Swampy, Eliza Loyie, Clifford Sinclair, and so many more. Worthy of special mention is Dorinda Kruger Allen, with whom I work and whose wisdom has brought me much insight and saved me from many missteps. I have learned so much about myself and my faith from these teachers who have taught and who are teaching me how to walk in a good way on this land.

I am also deeply grateful for my colleagues at Martin Luther University College (formerly Waterloo Lutheran Seminary) at Wilfrid Laurier University in Waterloo, ON, Canada. Special mention is owed some interlocutors there who have helped me much in this and related projects: Mona Tokarek LaFosse, Debbie Lou Ludolph, and Mary Philip (a.k.a. Joy). Thanks, as well, is owed to the two Principal-Deans whose tenures spanned this project and whose support made this possible: David Pfrimmer and Mark Harris. Gratitude is due to Harris Athanasiadis, whose reading of an earlier version of this monograph advanced it in important ways.

This project was supported, in part, by an Association of Theological Research Grant given to me for my sabbatical in the 2011–012 academic year. I am appreciative of ATS for this. Thanks is also due to the American Academy of Religion/Luce Foundation Summer Seminars on Comparative Theology and Theologies of Religious Pluralism project. I was a participant in this program for the summers of 2010 and 2011. I am grateful to those behind this initiative, with special mention to be made of John Thatamanil, who was Director of the Seminars. Thanks, as well, to both the anonymous reader whose suggestions immeasurably improved this book, and Alex Y Hwang, editor of the Religion and Borders series at Lexington, whose staff also deserve a word of gratitude. Thank you all.

Finally, I would be amiss not to express my gratitude to my family: my wife Gwenanne, and my daughters Anelise, Nadia, and Corin. These four strong women continue to inspire me and help me to become a better human being and theologian, in that order.

Introduction

LOCATING THEOLOGY

The city where I live was once called Berlin. In 1916, with Canada in the throes of the First World War, the city fathers thought it wise to rename it Kitchener, after the famous British soldier. Berlin had been a nod to the German heritage of my city, settled in the main by Mennonites coming north from Pennsylvania. These folk acquired land that once belonged to the Haudenosaunee, sometimes known as the Six Nations or the Iroquois, who were deeded six miles on each side of the Grand River, which flows through Kitchener.[1] The Six Nations of the Grand River Nation now own about 5 percent of their territory, deeded to them as compensation for lands lost due to their fidelity to the British Crown during the American Revolution. Its loss in Kitchener and beyond largely came about as a result of unscrupulous Indian Agents, who had a kind of power of attorney over the Haudenosaunee. They gave away some of this land to friends and relatives and sold some to pay their own wages. Some of the money from sales was used to establish a trust fund for the Haudenosaunee, which was lent out or invested by Crown agents, without a record of repayment or return on investment. Among that lost land is the lot upon which my house now sits, as well as the land upon which Martin Luther University College is located, where I work, and St. Matthews Lutheran Church, where I worship.

In this introduction I begin by locating myself because it has become increasingly clear to me that location matters. It matters because our locus holds stories: of creation, of fall, of redemption, and finally of hope. The stories that North America holds, this continent called Turtle Island by some of its First Nations, run deeper than the roughly 500 years since its "discovery." Settlers who now live in this territory know little of this long history, and also have a narrow repertoire of the stories from the last 500 years since contact. In this book, I hope to expand this a bit, first by attending to the stories and history recalled by the First Nations of this continent, but also by revisiting some of the stories we tell ourselves, stories of creation, sin, and redemption that we settlers have brought with us from Europe and other points. I write as a white Protestant (Lutheran) who is a second-generation immigrant. I am aware of my indebtedness to my forebears and so hold that tradition dearly and carefully. But I am becoming increasingly aware of the degree of indebtedness I hold to the Indigenous people who have stewarded Turtle Island. In what follows I strive to make some sense of "place" as a theological category (largely forgotten, or rejected, since the period called the Enlightenment) by starting where I am and engaging what I am learning from Indigenous people among whom I live as a settler: a student of Luther (a family friend whose wit, wisdom, and, sometimes, caustic style I have imbibed all of my life) and Schleiermacher (a dear friend from the days of my graduate studies). The matter to be discussed, then, is place and the stories about it that are told, or more often forgotten. The manner of dealing with this matter is methodologically that of comparative theology. In preparation for the present work, some comments on this methodology and its suitability for what follows are appropriate.

COMPARATIVE THEOLOGY: METHOD AND MORE

The term "comparative theology" has a long history, dating back to the 19th century.[2] And yet the task of comparing religions reaches back much further in Christianity. Ancient Christianity was attentive to "religious"[3] claims of other belief systems as worthy of consideration.[4] The history of Christianity, in part, is a story of the many varied ways that this comparison has been lived out in communities: sometimes with inquisitive interest, sometimes with hostile rebuke, but always with some degree of engagement insofar as "faith seeking understanding" always does so in particular places where others have ultimate experiences demanding of us an accounting of our experience over against theirs. We might count their experiences as valid, or incomplete, or illusory, or even demonic, but we will be pressed to make some sense of claims that encourage, contest, and deepen our own claims.

The use of "comparative theology" as a term in the 19th century really named something more akin to what would be called "religious studies" today. It was a methodology espousing a kind of rationality that critiqued confessionalism, deemed to be a fuel for religious wars of various sorts and antithetical to the vision espoused by proponents of "enlightenment."[5]

Today's theologians and religious studies scholars would both be skeptical about the use of "theology" to name this past phenomenon.

The term comparative theology was revived as it came to be used in North American in the late 20th century to reference the work of theologians committed to studying religious difference, convinced that deep learning in one religious tradition is enhanced by way of intentional engagement of other religious traditions in manners attentive to both convergence and divergence. This goal, then, eschewed and even today eschews the patterns of generalization and appeals to a priori understandings that underpinned the old comparative theology.[6] The pioneering 20th-century comparative theologians were especially invested in textual work, but as of late increasing interest in ritual, architecture, music, and so on have informed the comparative project.[7]

I first engaged comparative theology as a fellow of the AAR/Luce Summer Seminars in Comparative Theology and Theologies of Religious Pluralism in the years 2010 and 2011. Here, I learned—among many other things—that engaging another religious tradition enabled a fresh and enriched appreciation of my own. This learning shaped a sabbatical research project in the years 2011 and 2012 wherein I asked, "What might Christian theology learn from Indigenous spiritualities and worldviews?" The present work evolved from this project. It is important to note that I do not purport to write an Indigenous theology here, wherein I develop, illumine, or generate Indigenous thought. That is a task for Indigenous theologians. Rather, I intend to use insights I have humbly gained from generous Indigenous thinkers—Christian and not—to illumine a Christian theological locus: that of place. In preparation for this task, in what follows I underscore the contours of the comparative theology in the present work, wherein the reader will encounter a contextually informed theology that I name as autobiographical, circular, ethical-political, and generative in contour.

As noted above, the contextual reference for this particular work is my location on land deeded to the Haudenosaunee people. The Haudenosaunee are keepers of the Two-Row Wampum, which I will explore in more detail below.[8] At the heart of the teaching of the wampum is the idea that the Haudenosaunee and the Dutch were committed to living together in a respectful harmony with an appropriate distance between each people that allowed them space to live authentically. Dan Longboat explains the teaching as indicating that the wampum points to a sacred space that separates but conjoins people.[9] This teaching is informative for my understanding of comparative theology, which I will return to after considering the four contours noted above.

The first theme to be underscored is that of autobiography.[10] Frederick Buechner has written that "all theology, like all fiction, is at its heart autobiography."[11] This theme, of course, admits a variety of interpretations. At a very basic level, it reflects that theology has to do with me as an individual. In this sense, it might be said to draw upon the Reformation attention to the *pro me* character of the gospel. Yet more is understood and maintained by many theologians: the particular experiences that constitute my religious life are, in some fashion, revealing of the divine. Theology, then, is not solely about the passing on of information but about an encounter that shapes who I am yet in a fashion whereby I am the "expert" on this topic. No-one but me can write my experience: it demands an autobiography. It is my experience of eating at a Langar that allows me to see the Eucharist differently, and so I cannot assume that other people will draw the same conclusions. And yet, in this postmodern times, it would amiss to read this as if it were to be understood in a purely solipsistic fashion: the self is, in degrees, constructed.[12] There are forces and faces that have made me who I am, and that have made it possible for me to experience what I experience in this particular way or that. For this reason, an appeal to the autobiographical character of a comparative theology does not reduce theology to the experience of the self but instead attends to the self who experiences. This is a subtle but important distinction that warrants further discussion.

If "autobiography" is meant to focus on the experience of the self in the objective genitive, then the subject matter of theology is the self. The *extra nos* character of the theological enterprise is then too easily lost, and Feuerbach's critique of Christianity—and all religions really—is sustained.[13] One response to this is Barthian in nature. Here, the self is refused as the subject matter of theology and a theology of revelation is identified as a guarantor that privileges God as the divine subject matter. This is not an insignificant strategy, and it has borne some very important theological fruit.[14] And yet, a self that is eclipsed can too easily become a shadow self that skirts the illumination of the divine Word. The self is no longer necessary if theology is reduced to the talk of God alone and the idea that Love, or love, demands another is lost.[15] But then what becomes of this phantom self, or more importantly, what becomes of the Love loving the self? Such a Love is compromised as sovereignty rather than grace comes to the fore in our images of God.

If, however, the focus is on "the self who experiences" rather than the "experience of the self" then the self is first thought of as a subject of the act of intending an object. The phenomenon of our intending an object can be theologically analyzed. Consider, for instance, intention in the mode of desire. Here Rahner can help us in reminding that our desiring is grounded in the Desire that intends us. Beyond and behind each categorical, or historical, experience is a transcendental experience so profound and deep that it is found at the heart of all experience. Rahner labels this an *Urerlebnis*: a primordial experience of the divine beyond and behind and within all experiences.¹⁶ So, Rahner claims, our knowing God—and indeed our being known by God—arises in our experience of knowing what is not-God. The knowing and experiencing self, rather than the self per se, is the means of divine illumination. This is pertinent for a comparative theology because it invites the theologian to ponder all experiences as sites of divine revelation.¹⁷ This, then, occasions the possibility for understanding interreligious experience as possibly revelatory. In the present work I draw heavily on such experiences, especially those experiences I have of encountering the religious other in Indigenous spiritualities and worldviews.

This book finds much fodder for theology thought in my interaction with Indigenous individuals, communities, and their lives together. The presupposition that is operative here is that these experiences of interaction are data for theological reflection. Moreover, this data includes the experience of vulnerability intrinsic in multiple religious participation.¹⁸ The self is deeply engaged in these experiences, which involve both risk and loneliness.¹⁹ This is why comparative theology has been compared to pilgrimage.²⁰ The self is in a journey toward the divine and finds the self along the way: a kind of collateral benefit. The self that comes around to find itself anew speaks to this method's circular character, the second contour mentioned above.

The motif of the cyclical nature of reality looms large in Indigenous thought and practice. Kidwell, Noley, and Tinker note that Indigenous people "lived their lives in accordance with the cycles of nature," although it is to be noted that this theme is not universal among Indigenous peoples.²¹ Mircea Eliade proposed that for ancient peoples, sacred time was circular.²² The circle as a symbol, then, is significant for certain Indigenous groups. Margaret Kovach develops a Nêhiýaw/Plains Cree research methodology that is envisioned as circular in nature, reflecting the importance of the circular for her community.²³ Anishinaabe scholar Kathy Absolon notes that "We will hear people say that our methodologies exist in our dreams, in our fast ... by community forums, by sitting in circles and by engaging in ceremony."²⁴

Across the Great Plains, people will be familiar with the circularity of the teepee rings. Medicine wheels communicate holistic life as circular and speak to the Indigenous experience of coming around again to where you were— whether in time or space or the cycles of life. Indigenous author/poet Leanne Simpson notes that she has a perennial argument with her editors, who want to correct her propensity to re-use phrases and paragraphs in a given work.²⁵ She refuses to bend, however, noting that re-iteration is a part of Indigenous pedagogy. Stories are told and retold in order that they might permeate the being of the hearer. This strategy, of course, is not unique to Indigenous communities. The ancient Christian tradition of the church year sets the stories of the people of faith in a cycle that enables the formation of the faithful by way of repetition. Moreover, this practice is a part of many, if not most, religious traditions. This cyclic proclivity, of course, echoes the cycles of nature and so reflects that our spiritual journeys are not to be abstracted from our experiences of the created order.

The kind of comparative theology to be encountered in this book, then, is one in which attention to the circle also means attention to the globe, and so creation proper. This attention to creation will serve as a significant point of contact for Indigenous insights and a chastened Christianity. The adjective "chastened" here is significant insofar as Christianity has too easily been co-opted by the cult of progress that has accompanied the advance of Christian theology in the modern era. Vítor Westhelle wrote of the need for a re-invigorated eschatology that imagines a re-appropriation of the role of place in the Christian imaginary.[26] At the heart of this corrective is a refusal of the modern fixation with progress that has seen the category of place usurped by that of time, and more pointedly, by time in a particular modality that is linear.[27] The ancients, living in close harmony with the earth, knew time primarily as cyclical even while they were also able to appreciate that time also moved forward. Many contemporary Indigenous communities hold this ancient knowledge still today, recognizing the danger of wholly linear perspectives.[28]

A comparative theology that is circular then will be iterative. Its cyclical character functions as a rhetorical strategy for both pedagogic and aesthetic aims. The art of rhetoric recalls the medieval conviction of the Greek transcendental of beauty, which, together with truth and goodness, constitutes a unity: truth, beauty, and goodness are convertible.[29] They advance together to the end that fullness of life obtains in the life of the philosopher, that is, the one who loves wisdom. The Socratic method, of course, made much of circularity and iteration to achieve the wisdom that shines through truth, beauty, and the good. Wisdom, of course, is a watchword for the comparative theologian. Consider the following from John Thatamanil:

> I have argued elsewhere that our era requires a "new kind of wisdom: the capacity to see the world through more than one set of religious lenses and to integrate into one life, insofar as possible, what is disclosed through lenses. . . . For lack of a better phrase, I call this binocular wisdom, an extension from binocular vision, vision generated by both eyes, the only kind that yields depth perspective."[30]

Thatamanil here references the need for viewing phenomena from more than one religious perspective in order to better one's vision in attaining wisdom. "Vision" is an important word here that invites us to consider this wisdom as informed by and informing the "ideas" (from the Greek word for "forms") of truth, beauty, and goodness. A comparative theologian, then, is not only attentive to various religious insights but also attentive to the aesthetic of religious life which is especially evident as we look both across the religions and deep within any one religion. Comparison is not only about ideas but about the ideas/forms that "take place" in the circularity of religious life.

The circularity of religious life, then, is a strategy that aims at truth and goodness by way of an aesthetic engagement of the fullness of the human experience in "stalking the divine."[31] Circularity is a commitment to keep coming back to the subject at hand for the sake of fullness. And so, circularity is not about mere repetition, but repetition for the sake of advance. Moreover, a circularity done in good faith is one that experiences something of the aesthetic abandon of the artist, or perhaps the dancer of the powwow circle, if not the hora, or that of the whirling dervish. Examples multiply because the circle is an existential of being human even while certain rehearsals of modernity reject it in favor of the trajectory.[32]

The circle, then, informs the autobiographical by underscoring that we never leave behind where we have been but return to it with new insights. There is, then, an intrinsically hermeneutical character to the task of comparative theology.[33] A new insight enables us to receive what we already have in a new light. The task of autobiography, as an intrinsic human task, is well served by comparative theology insofar as it commends us to take the deep learnings we have enjoyed from our religious traditions/experiences and revisit them in light of illuminations accorded by another religious tradition. The circle, it seems, allows me to take what I have to the other and to take what the other has given me back to myself. In a fashion, both the strange are made familiar and the familiar are made strange by the circle. The circle is a cipher for the dialect of the strange and familiar: we never really know what is familiar to us until it has been problematized, and we can never recognize the strange unless something familiar in it calls out to us. Comparative theology, then, is circular in that it works through this dialectic to the dual ends of better understanding religious expressions that exist and in expressing new understandings of religious existence. And yet it must be underscored that this task both holds and identifies possible dangers as we circle toward and within the good. Comparative theology, then, is an ethical-political task. We turn now to consider this.

From the outset, it is important to return to the theme of the convertibility of the transcendentals: truth, goodness, and beauty advance together—distinguished but never divorced from one another. As we consider the phenomena of religious life, we know that insofar as they are true and beautiful, they also aim at the good. In modernity, ordered by the Enlightenment, the good holds a kind of religious trump card. We see this in particular in the legacy of Kant, whose "Religion within the Limits of Reason," outlines moral canons for the truth of religion.[34] Practically, this has resulted in a vision of religion in the West wherein the presumption is that religions are problems unless wrested into the confines of the personal.[35] This construction of the secular stands in stark contrast to secularism in India, for instance, where it is a social commitment (in theory, if not in fact) to guarantee space for a plurality of religious voices in the public sphere.[36] There have been, of course, important voices contradicting the predominant narrative of this Western view of secularism, underscoring that religious life has and remains a thick contribution—in various modalities—to the public in its Western iterations.[37] The long and short of this is pluralism, often understood as a religious problem in the West. Political theorists and armchair philosophers have underscored this in terms of the recurring phenomenon of religious wars in their various forms. In response to these critiques of religion, as well as in response to the simple need to provide an accounting of the phenomenon of religious plurality, theologies of religious pluralism loom large in theological curricula.

Paul Knitter and John Hick are especially prominent and early voices that have done much to advance the conversation regarding theologies of religious pluralism. Most students of theology will be familiar with their paradigms of exclusivism, universalism, and pluralism as a means whereby they name the tendencies of religions to see their truth claims to be exclusive of others, inclusive of others, or parallel to others.[38] S. Mark Heim has advanced the idea that different religions have different religious ends as a further option for pondering a phenomenology of the religions.[39] For the purposes of this work, I will name this as particularism in contracts to exclusivism, universalism, and pluralism.

Francis X. Clooney asserts that comparative theology and theologies of religious pluralism mirror, imply, and help one another.[40] I would affirm this and simply add that it is an ethical imperative for theologians to name how they account for religious pluralism even while they go about the task of comparing theologies, or religious worldviews. This is an especially important and pertinent task in the present case. Christians have too often engaged other religious traditions in the guise of condemnation or appropriation. The former is especially hideous, while the latter is dangerous in an insidious modality. Consider the following recommendation from the Osage theologian George "Tink" Tinker as he ponders the interest of Christians in Indigenous traditions as they search to correct spirituality run amok in the West:

> I would encourage our amer-european relatives to find another way to find their own center of balance rather than invading our ceremonies and imposing their presence on Indian communities at moments of ceremonial intimacy. Indeed, there is unfinished business that deeply affects the spiritual well-being of our White relatives that calls out for attention today.[41]

In North America (and beyond) the history of settlers and the Indigenous is one of the invaders robbing the people of the land of their territories, of their sovereignty, of their children—forced into residential and boarding schools, of their treaties in duplicitous treatment, of their language in the colonial reach of English, and so forth. It is quite understandable that some Indigenous people are rather suspicious of Christian interest in their ceremonies. The problem of appropriation looms large in the pondering the task of comparative theology between Christianity and Indigenous traditions. In my estimation, particularism best respects the integrity of each in this asymmetrical relationship. It is more amenable to respecting the principle of the Two-Row Wampum, I think.

The Two-Row Wampum is an instance of the broader practice of treaty-making across Turtle Island. The importance of understanding treaties properly cannot be underestimated. Settlers too often understand treaties to be legal documents regarding matters reduced to material consequence. Cardinal and Hildebrandt note that a proper understanding of treaties must begin with "spiritual foundations underlying the treaty making process."[42] Treaties are understood to be living documents grounded in relationship to the Creator, with the intent of giving First Nations the right to maintain "relationships with the Creator through the laws given to them by Him."[43] Treaties include an irrevocable commitment to peace and presume the establishment of a relationship more akin to familial than any other.[44] The common understanding of treaty in the mind of settlers fails to appreciate an Indigenous apprehension of treaties as including oral stories, eyewitness accounts, articles of treaties, etc.[45] Treaties are, finally, proof that Indigenous people negotiated with federal government representatives on a nation-to-nation basis.[46] In sum, imagining comparative theology as analogous to treaty-making presumes that the theologian respects the identity, the dignity, and independence of religious traditions even while realizing that the commitment to cross religious boundaries and to be received, and to receive those from other traditions is evidence of the fact that comparative theology is fundamentally a relational endeavor. The Two-Row Wampum was an instance of a treaty presuming the independence of both the Haudenosaunee and the Dutch, and the relationship entered into by the vehicle of that treaty.

Of course, it would be misleading to paint a picture in which North America consists of white Christians and Indigenous Traditionalists. In fact, many Indigenous people identify with Christianity, even while some practice rituals in both traditions. These, then, could be examples of multiple religious belonging. As a settler Christian, however, this is not an option for me. I cannot belong to an Indigenous Nation—apart from the highly unusual instance of being adopted into one—and so cannot practice multiple religious belonging with those who practice Indigenous traditions. I can and have, however, participated in Indigenous traditions when invited. For this reason, the distinction between multiple religious belonging and multiple religious participation is highly important for settler co-religionists with Indigenous spiritual practitioners, and the latter is the only ethical option, in my estimation.[47]

In sum, then, as I put Indigenous insights and Christian theology into a conversation regarding place, I do so with a theology of religious pluralism that is particularist in nature and that looks to a language of multiple religious participation rather than belonging. These decisions are largely driven by the ethical reality that I engage a spiritual perspective that has experienced too much appropriation by Christians.[48] But this latter is also an important piece of data that a comparative theology must attend to with the result that comparative theology in this conversation, in good faith, is necessarily political as well.

Hugh Nicolson, in discussing comparative theology, notes that the 19th-century comparativists sought to de-politicize theology.[49] And yet he notes that religions form by structuring via social groups that necessarily imply some level of exclusion—"distinction" might be more helpful.[50] Various attempts to give an accounting of religious life in abstraction from this seemingly problematic of piety largely have failed. In fact, Nicholson asserts that "the attempt to liberate religious commitment from exclusionary attitudes toward other communities often only results in more subtle and insidious forms of exclusion."[51] This might well be used to name how many Indigenous people the world round have experienced Christianity under the tutelage of empire: in the name of the one who embodied tolerance and inclusion we have usurped the agency of Indigenous peoples.[52] There arises, then, in the present context the call to people of all faiths to respect the particular religious ends and sovereignty of all faith, but most especially that of Indigenous peoples.[53] Creating the condition for the possibility of exclusion (or distinction), then, is a political act whereby we allow for the other to clarify their identity vis-à-vis ours in such a way that something like authentic tolerance can be achieved.[54] The present work remains committed to this as both a hermeneutic for reading across these two traditions and a strategy for articulating Christian responsibility as global citizens with a commitment to justice, or the good as a phenomenon that necessarily emerges with beauty and truth. We turn now to the latter of these in considering the generative nature of comparative theology.

The fourth contour of comparative theology that is of some consequence for the present work is its generative capacity. In the quotation from John Thatamanil noted above, he cited the need for a binocular wisdom.[55] In this context he also spoke of how this duality creates a tension that is generative. As beauty and goodness advance, so does truth, and for this reason, we can anticipate that a method of comparative theology will generate truth—even while it is always a truth to be contested and tried in the crucible of personal experience and under the tutelage of communal experiences as attested in the hermeneutical circle of engaging scripture and traditional ceremonies.

In the task of comparative theology under exploration here, it is to be noted that a kind of asymmetry obtains insofar as Indigenous traditions do not typically draw upon written texts in the same manner that we find to be the case with Christianity. What are we to make of this? Does this then become an asymmetry whereby Christianity has a kind of trump card, or not, because of its reliance on textual sources? I think not, and I come to that conclusion because of four sub-themes I want to explore before discussing the generative capacity of this exercise of comparative theology.

First, we too often imagine—in Protestant theology—that scripture is a kind of other to ritual and ceremony. The permanence of scripture stands over against the contextual and temporal plasticity of ritual, storytelling, etc. Such a judgment errs in both over-estimating the fixity of texts and under-estimating the power and permanence of ritual and orality. Moreover, the texts that Christians read include extended pieces that are concretizations of earlier performed oral traditions as well as written text meant to be orally performed.[56] Consequently, Christians, too, are invested in orality in the communication of religious truths.

Second, Protestants often imagine the reading of scripture to be an experience in individuality. And yet the very task of reading is communal in nature. Moreover, the very texts we read are expressions of the communal experiences, transmitted in communities and translated by languages that are always constructs of communities. The original Hebrew, Aramaic, and Greek of the Christian Bible are communal products and the English or Malayalam into which we translate them are also communally construed. Reading is always an exercise in translating meaning in the context of community. This same obtains in Indigenous traditions. At a panel discussion on the topic of teaching theology with a view toward truth and reconciliation between settler and Indigenous communities, the question was asked about what constitutes Indigenous spirituality.[57] Murray Pruden, a Cree participant in the audience, answered the question by noting that Indigenous spirituality is about the language of the people.[58] Languages bear us and speak us as much as we speak them. This is true whether it is the case that the language in question is written or spoken or sung. But what is it that language does? This brings me to my third thought on the text versus ceremony question.

The Indigenous author Thomas King writes, "The truth about stories is that that's all we are."[59] Despite the desire of many to articulate truth claims propositionally, this turn to story is perhaps most cogent. Stories have a profound capacity to illumine truth indirectly and so substantially. Stories get at the evasive nature of truth, and its trickster character. Stories and truth poke fun at us and teach us not to take ourselves too seriously, and so to take truth more seriously. Truth in the guise of stories reminds us that how we tell a story affects what the story does. The aesthetic of a story shapes the praxis of its consequence: stories shape us into people who do truth, rather than into people who own the truth. For this reason, both the Christian theology and the Indigenous ceremonies and stories that we will explore in what follows take as a starting point the conviction that putting Christian scripture and tradition alongside Indigenous narrative and ceremony finds a meeting point in the truth that stories are what we are. These stories told in the give and take of comparative theology are, I believe, generative.[60]

John Thatamanil notes that religions advance both comprehensive worldviews and qualitative orientations funded by "interpretive schemes and therapeutic regimes."[61] In short, religions make truth claims that are framed contextually and facilitate change. In comparative theology, claims of various traditions are set alongside one another. This provides the possibility for what Arvind Sharma calls "reciprocal illumination," which he contrasts with the task of religious comparison identified with the work of W.B. Kristensen, Gerardus van der Leeuw, and Mircea Eliade:

> Comparison is often employed to draw general conclusions based on material drawn from different religious traditions, and the conclusion drawn could well transcend the self-understanding of the believers themselves. The concept of reciprocal illumination possesses a more limited focus and embodies the idea that something in an other religious tradition (or other traditions) may help us understand something in our own religious tradition more profoundly and clearly, and vice versa.[62]

Two points warrant consideration here: first, I consider it too narrow to imagine that this reciprocal illumination only illumines what is already present in my religious tradition, although it does accomplish that. Comparative theology (which more nearly approximates Sharma's reciprocal illumination than does comparative religious studies, I think) is, as James Fredericks notes, constructive in character.[63] And yet, following Sharma and Nicolson, the propensity of the illumination that comes from setting religious traditions alongside each other is of a character that ought to resist generalization so as to make its generative claims contextual in character. Does this utterly relativize religious or intra-religious claims to the end that they cannot offer a comprehensive worldview? I want to suggest that the universal claims made in the crucible of interreligious illumination are modest in character insofar as they evolve in the context of a conversation that may not be easily translatable to another context—or perhaps cannot be translated to another context. In a fashion, then, the insights generated by engaging Christian theology and Indigenous spiritualties and worldviews will be circumscribed by the Indigenous notion that ceremonies take place *in situ*.[64] The truth of a ceremony is circumscribed by its location. The truth generated by the practice of comparative theology, then, is a situated truth. Truth appears indirectly in truths *in situ*, and so invites us to think of place anew, the very intention of this work.

In sum, it is to be noted that the comparative theology exercised here is done with the intention of constructing a theology of place. The turn to place in modern academic discourse is beyond the scope of the present work.[65] My efforts to address this will draw on insights from this discourse, in an ad hoc fashion. What follows is my attempt to provide some contours to a response to this question, located between my confessional identity and my own engagement of Indigenous insights—a phenomenon too often disparaged on Turtle Island. In response to this neglect, I start the present work with attention to the First Peoples of this place, anticipating that they will raise issues of critical importance for a theology of place for a settler's perspective. The present work does not intend to develop or appropriate an Indigenous understanding of place, but to garner from Indigenous insights a perspective for a non-dominant reading of Luther and Schleiermacher in service of a theology of place. It is at the border-land meeting point of Christianity and Indigenous spirituality that I look for rich resources for developing a contextually appropriate settler theology of place on Turtle Island.

In the first chapter I note that in the context of North America, perhaps no assertion is as demanding of an apologetic riposte as Vine Deloria Jr.'s conviction that a proper religion needs a land of its own. While Christian might eschew such a claim in light of their affirmation of Christianity as a landless—and so universal—religion, its collusion with empires that have land thirst can be seen as evidence to the contrary. In this chapter I engage the insights of Indigenous voices to the end that Christian dependence—and denial of that dependence—on land, place, and space is brought into relief to the end that a recognition and reconstrual of our relationship to place (as a broader catch-term for the three) is renewed. Of some import, in Indigenous understandings of place, is that certain locations are spiritually intense. I use the phrase "kairotic places" to name these.

In the second chapter, I consider Luther's theology, which when read in concert with Indigenous insights invites his students to attend to certain key themes with special interest in questions of place. Luther is read with this spatial hermeneutic, thereby rejecting temptations to treat him as preoccupied with linear time—as if he were a modern subject obsessed with progress. Instead, I attend to Luther's deep appreciation of place, which is evident in his rich theology of creation. This is often occluded by modern readers invested in post-Kantian preoccupations with the subject. Luther saw God's poetic work in creation, and by placing this in conversation with Indigenous insights it is affirmed that kairotic places are kenotic in that God artfully gives over the divine self in creation and crafts in us care for the other that is kenotic in character.

Schleiermacher is put in conversation with Indigenous insights in the third chapter. In so doing, the following motifs emerge: particular places become profoundly potent in awakening us to the truth of space and the potency latent in it; place can, in certain instances, be deemed non-competitive and so commending the practice of hospitality; and particular places can serve as ciphers for our apprehension of the whole, and so serve as an occasion for our healing as we find ourselves ushered into a vision of the Reign of God wherein harmony is given to us as the sine qua non of that peace which provides sustenance in life. Kairotic places, then, are harmonic and as such, hospitable and healing.

The fourth chapter serves as a constructive moment in this work in further exploring how certain places are kairotic in poetic potency. While some identify sites as sacred by fiat, or perhaps convention, I propose that they can be ephemerally sacred under the aegis of the Spirit. Such kairotic places remind us that re-creation is not the obliteration of creation, but its re-construal to the end that we experience the earth as a Mother who births us into a new kind of agency. The land, then, is our relative and we live authentically when we live in harmony with it and are shaped by its contours. Certain places, then, make plain that we do not give up ourselves in giving ourselves away but, like the earth, finally come to be most fully in giving away who we are as we give in love. Such places are "kairotic" and enable us to take all places seriously, and thereby facilitate an encounter with the holy to take place.

In conclusion, I propose that kairotic places are liminal in character and so most often found at the margins, where we experience hope as we despair of our own capacities. This obtains, too, of the religions. At the edges of each religion, interfaith encounters make possible the experience of sacred hope. In response to insights from Indigenous interlocutors, I explore a secular vision of hope, described by Dominique Moïsi as a mode of confidence in the face of upheaval before exploring a theological understanding of hope under the tutelage of Karl Rahner. In conversation with Indigenous thinkers whose experience across religious traditions is informative and in reflecting on an experience I had while sojourning on the Great Plains, I explore my experience of hope's location at the kairos of the margins—most specifically the margins of interfaith encounters—that enable us to understand both interfaith realities and the demands of faithfulness.

NOTES

1. For a brief history of this, see "Six Miles Deep: Land Rights of the Six Nations of the Grand River," Six Nations of the Grand River Nation, accessed March 08, 2020, http://www.sixnations.ca/SixMilesDeepBooklet2015Final.pdf.

2. Nicolson, *Comparative Theology and the Problem of Religious Rivalry* (Oxford: Oxford University Press, 2011), 25.

3. I put this adjective in quotation marks in this first instance, mindful that in what follows the word "religion" and its variants can only be applied to ancient belief systems anachronistically. "Religious" in medieval Christianity, for instance, referenced "anyone living under canonical vows of poverty, chastity and obedience in a community and under a rule." Geddes M. MacGregor, *Dictionary of Religion and Philosophy* (New York: Paragon House, 1991), 533. There is no consensus on the use of the word in contemporary parlance. John Bowker in "Religion," in *Oxford Concise Dictionary of World Religions*, ed. John Bowker (Oxford: Oxford University Press, 2005) characterizes "religion" using a cluster of markers including ethics, text, tradition, story, myth, ritual, and symbol. He notes that we "can recognize a religion when we see one because we know that many characteristics are; but we would not expect to find any religion which exhibited all the characteristics without exception" (xxx). Thomas Tweed in *Crossing and Dwelling: A Theory of Religion* (Cambridge, MA: Harvard, 2008), 54 proposes a locative definition of religion that would be hospitable to Indigenous traditions, even while Indigenous elders and so on more generally eschew "religion" as encompassing their practice: "Religions are confluences of organic-cultural flows that intensify joy and confront suffering by drawing on human and superhuman forces to make homes and cross boundaries." Peter Beyer in *Religions and Global Society* (Abingdon: Routledge, 2006), 4, 5 opts for a sociological approach. He shies away from functional definitions of a religion (what it does) and argues more for a substantive definition of religion (what it is) although in a manner in which social location softens universal claims. For the present work the operating understanding of religion will be as follows: religion references a system of practices informing and informed by belief systems making ultimate claims. See Roy C. Amore and Amil Hussain, "About Religion," in *A Concise Introduction to World Religions: Third Edition*, eds. Willard G. Oxtoby, Roy C. Amore, Amir Hussain, and Alan F. Segal (Oxford: Oxford University Press, 2015), which informs my working definition. I am grateful to Dr. Jason Neelis for helpful conversation in regard to the necessary perils in defining "religion."

4. John Thatamanil, "Eucharist Upstairs, Yoga Downstairs: On Multiple Religious Participation," in *Many Yet One? Multiple Religious Belonging*, eds. Peniel Jesudason Rufus Rajkumar and Joseph Prabhakar Dayam (Geneva: World Council of Churches, 2016), 6.

5. Nicolson, *Comparative Theology and Religious Rivalry*, 25. See Immanuel Kant, "An Answer to the Question: What is Enlightenment?" in *Practical Philosophy, The Cambridge Edition of the Works of Immanuel Kant*, ed. Mary J. Gregor (Cambridge: Cambridge University Press, 1996) for a very fine summary of this movement in early modernity.

6. Nicolson, *Comparative Theology and Religious Rivalry*, 29.

7. See for instance, A Bagus Laksana, "Comparative Theology: Between Identity and Alterity," in *The New Comparative Theology: Interreligious Insights from the Next Generation*, ed. Francis X. Clooney, S.J. (London: T&T Clark, 2003), 2–19 who uses pilgrimage to point to third spaces as points of interreligious encounters.

8. The Two-Row Wampum is an agreement made between the Haudenosaunee and Dutch, and is "scripted" in a beaded scroll that is two purple stripes against a white background. The rows represent two rivers, one traveled on by the Dutch, and the other by the Haudenosaunee, with the understanding that they travel together, but on their own path. The image on the cover of this book is a picture of a replica of one I made at a wampum belt making workshop titled "Creation and Clan Story Workshops Featuring George Kennedy" at Toronto Council Fire Native Cultural Centre, August 21–23, 2018.

9. Dan Longboat, "Hodinohso:ni Ecological Knowledge and the Dish with One Spoon Conversation in Cultural Fluency #2 Conference," YouTube, October 2015, https://www.youtube.com/watch?v=e5szQHeQ9FM.

10. Francis X. Clooney, S.J., "Response," in *The New Comparative Theology*, 199.

11. Frederick Buechner, *The Sacred Journey: A Memoir of Early Days* (New York: Harper Collins, 1991).

12. See Homi K. Bhaba, "Interrogating Identity: Franz Fanon and the Postcolonial Prerogative," in *The Location of Culture* (Hoboken: Taylor and Francis, 2012), 57–93; Gayatri Chakravorty Spivak, "Can the Subaltern Speak?" in *Can the Subaltern Speak: Reflections on the History of an Idea*, ed. Rosalind Morris (New York: Columbia University Press, 2010), 66–71; Jean-François Lyotard, *The Post-Modern Explained* (Minneapolis: University of Minnesota Press, 1992), 20, 21.

13. Ludwig Feuerbach, *The Essence of Christianity*, ed. George Eliot (Buffalo, NY: Prometheus Books, 1989).

14. The Barmen Declaration, for example, is a document that is marked by Barth's "Nein" to religious capitulation to the self, writ large in this instance. See *Creeds of the Churches*, 3rd ed., ed. John H. Leith (Louisville, KY: Anchor Books, 1982), 517–21.

15. This is clearly not Barth's intention yet it persists as a danger in theologies that refuse the possibility that God suffers human and cosmic activity. Love is always suffering since those who love are both agents and patients.

16. Karl Rahner, S.J., *Schriften zur Theologie IX* (Zürich: Benzinger, 1970), 169.

17. This turn allows attention to the plurality of forces operative in and upon me while it also underscores that I alone have front seat in this experience. I am, at a fundamental level, the one best able to bear witness to my sense of disjuncture that is so often a central part of the experience of encountering the religious other.

18. Simone Sinn, "Vulnerability and Agency in Multiple Religious Belonging: Or, Why God Matters," in *Many Yet One?*, 68.

19. Laksana, "Comparative Theology," 10.

20. Ibid., 3.

21. See Clara Sue Kidwell, Homer Noley, and George E. Tinker, *A Native American Theology* (New York: Orbis Books, 2002), 13.

22. Mircea Eliade, *The Sacred and the Profane: The Nature of Religion* (Boston, MA: Mariner Book, 2001), 70, 110.

23. Margaret Kovach, *Indigenous Methodologies: Characteristics, Conversations, and Contexts* (Toronto: University of Toronto Press, 2009), 44, 45.

24. Cited in Kovach, *Indigenous Methodologies*, 126.

25. Leanne Simpson, "Decolonial Love, Indigenous Resurgence and the Art of Living Justly" (lecture, Wilfrid Laurier University, Waterloo, ON, December 2, 2015).

26. Vítor Westhelle, *Eschatology and Space* (New York: Palgrave MacMillan, 2012), 27.

27. See Edward W. Soja, *Postmodern Geographies: The Reassertion of Space in Critical Social Theory* (New York: Verso, 1989), 27 who notes that historicism silences space.

28. Rupert Ross, *Dancing with a Ghost: Exploring Aboriginal Reality* (Toronto: Penguin, 2006), 186.

29. Wouter Goris and Jan Aertsen, "Medieval Theories of Transcendentals," in *Stanford Encyclopedia of Philosophy (Online)*, accessed August, 28, 2018, https://plato.stanford.edu/entries/transcendentals-medieval/.

30. Thatamanil, "Eucharist Upstairs, Yoga Downstairs," 20.

31. Paul Tillich describes art (along with philosophy) as an indirect means by which we "experience and express ultimate reality" and religion as a direct means. See "Art and Ultimate Reality," in *Art, Creativity, and the Sacred*, ed. Diane Apostolos-Cappadona (New York: Continuum, 1998), 221. The term "stalking the divine" comes from Kristen Ohlson, *Stalking the Divine: Contemplating Faith with the Poor Claires* (New York: Hachette Books, 2003).

32. Charles Taylor distinguishes what he calls "higher time" from "secular time." The latter is chronological in character, whereas in the former "Good Friday 1998 is closer in a way to the original day of the Crucifixion than mid-summer's day 1997." See *A Secular Age* (Cambridge, MA: Harvard University Press, 2007), 55. This move funds a social imaginary in the modern age that is drastically different from both that of ancient Christianity and that of Indigenous worldviews, I would add. See ibid, 459ff.

33. See James Fredericks, in "Introduction," *The New Comparative Theology*, xii who notes that comparative theology is both constructive and hermeneutical.

34. Immanuel Kant, *Religion Within the Limits of Reason Alone*, eds. Theodore M. Greene and Hoyt H. Hudson (New York: Harper, 1960).

35. Taylor, *A Secular Age*, 588–590.

36. Sunder John Boopalan, "Hybridity's Ambiguity (Gift or Threat?): Marginality as Rudder," *Many Yet One?*, 135.

37. See for instance Robert A. Orsi, *History and Presence* (Cambridge, MA: The Belknap Press of Harvard University Press, 2016).

38. See *Christian Approaches to Other Faiths*, eds. Alan Race and Paul Hedges (London: SCM Press, 2008), 36–110 for a fine introduction to these.

39. S. Mark Heim, *Salvations: Truth and Difference in Religion* (Maryknoll, NY: Orbis Books, 1995); *The Depth of the Riches: A Trinitarian Theology of Religious Ends* (Grand Rapids, MI: Eerdmans, 2001).

40. Clooney, "Response," 196.

41. George E. Tinker, *American Indian Liberation: A Theology of Sovereignty* (Maryknoll, NY: Orbis Books, 2008), 141.

42. Harold Cardinal and W. Hildebrandt, *Treaty Elders of Saskatchewan: Our Dream Is That Our People Will One Day be Clearly Recognized as Nations* (Calgary: University of Calgary Press, 2000), 1.

43. Ibid., 6–7.

44. Ibid., 32, 34.

45. Ibid., 50.

46. Ibid., 58.

47. See Thatamanil, "Eucharist Upstairs, Yoga Downstairs," 10; See also Hans Gustafson, "Descandalizing Multiple Religious Identity with Help from Nicholas Black Elk and His Spirituality: An Exercise in Interreligious Learning," *Journal of Ecumenical Studies* 51, no. 1 (Winter 2016): 80–113 and Michelle Voss Roberts, "Religious Belonging and the Multiple," *Journal of Feminist Studies in Religion* 26, no. 1 (2010): 43–62.

48. Further to note 3 above: the ambiguous term "religion" is largely eschewed by traditional practitioners of Indigenous ceremonies etc. Religion is considered a European word that does not adequately name the fullness of Indigenous practices, which are deemed to be so holistic as to refute the Western tendency to compartmentalize life. Notwithstanding Christian critiques of this very practice, in respect for Indigenous practitioners, I will refrain from describing Indigenous ceremonies etc. as "religions" even while recognizing that terms such as multiple religious participation name the phenomena of experiencing the spiritual resources of both baptism and the smudge, for example. See also Voss Roberts, *op cit.* for a discussion of how the term "belonging" fails to account for some phenomena of the lived experience of religious identity.

49. Nicholson, *Comparative Theology and Religious Rivalry*, xii.

50. Ibid., 51.

51. Ibid., 79.

52. Again, the history of the residential and board schools in Canada and United States are significant examples of this. See "They Came for the Children" for more on this. Further to this see Truth and Reconciliation Commission of Canada, *They Came for the Children: Canada, Aboriginal Peoples, and Residential Schools* (Winnipeg: Truth and Reconciliation Commission of Canada, 2012).

53. See the *United Nations Declaration on the Rights of Indigenous Peoples* for an important summary of work to be done across the globe in partnership with Indigenous peoples. The document can be located at United Nations, accessed August 28, 2018, https://www.un.org/esa/socdev/unpfii/documents/DRIPS_en.pdf.

54. Nicholson, *Comparative Theology and Religious Rivalry*, 80.

55. See note 27 above. See also David Ford, *Shaping Theology: Engagements in a Religious and Secular World* (Malden, MA: Blackwell Publishing, 2007), xvii, who identifies wisdom as that which embraces the imaginative, intellectual, passionate and practical.

56. I am grateful to my colleague Mona Tokarek LaFosse for conversations regarding this insight. She has helped me to see, in particular, the power of orality in performing scripture, and its grounding in the early church's understanding of

texts. For an example of this insight at work, see Mona Tokarek LaFosse, "Those Who Hear: The Power of Learners in 1 Timothy," in *Religions and Education in Antiquity: Studies in Honour of Michel Desjardins*, ed. Alex Damm (Leiden: Brill, 2019), 147–170. For another example of an important work applying orality in biblical exegesis see David Rhoads, Joanna Dewey and Donald Michie, *Mark as Story: Introduction to the Narrative of a Gospel, Third Edition* (Minneapolis, MN: Fortress Press, 2012).

57. Allen G. Jorgenson, Mona Tokarek LaFosse, Debbie Lou Ludolph, and Mary (Joy) Philip, "Respecting Indigenous Spirituality in Its Own Right" (panel, Canadian Theological Society, Regina, SK, May 28, 2018).

58. In latter correspondence with Murray regarding this, he noted, "Our language is the connection to the land. It is the language of our Mother Earth. This is how we speak to her. In essence, a way we talk and pray to God our Creator as well. When so many Indigenous children were taken away from their communities and families because of the residential school system, they were taken away from their culture. Along with that, [came] a loss of our language, the communication to the land, to our Mother. This becomes a generational degradation to the children, grandchildren and great grandchildren, the loss of our spiritual connection and language to our Mother. This is our sacred and spiritual nature to the land and we are at a threshold and a drastic time of losing that spiritual connection to the land but also our voice as a people." Murray Pruden, email correspondence, March 19, 2019.

59. Thomas King, *The Truth About Stories: A Native Narrative* (Toronto: Anansi Press, 2003), 2.

60. Note as well the Indigenous reticence to make sense of stories told. Shawn Wilson notes that a storyteller will not explain his or her story since to do so would dishonor hearers: *Research Is Ceremony: Indigenous Research Methods* (Winnipeg: Fernwood, 2008), 135.

61. Thatamanil, "Eucharist Upstairs, Yoga Downstairs," 14.

62. Arvind Sharma, "Reciprocal Illumination," in *Interreligious Comparisons in Religious Studies and Theology*, eds. Perry Schmidt-Leukel and Andreas Nehring (New York: Bloomsbury, 2016), 181.

63. Fredericks, "Introduction," *The New Comparative Theology*, xii.

64. Basil Johnston, *The Manitous* (St. Paul: The Minnesota Historical Society, 2001), 6. See Vine Deloria Jr., *Custer Died for Your Sins: An Indian Manifesto* (Norman: Oklahoma University Press, 1988), 179.

65. A very fine introduction to this is found in Tim Cresswell, *Place: An Introduction*, 2nd ed. (Malden, MA: Wiley Blackwell, 2015). Of critical importance is the aforementioned Soja, *Postmodern Geographies: The Reassertion of Space in Critical Social Theory*. See also Gaston Bachelard, *The Poetics of Space*, trans. Maria Jolas (Boston, MA: Beacon Press, 1958). Richard Kearney and Brian Treanor (eds.), *Carnal Hermeneutics* (New York: Fordham, 2015); Jacques Derrida, *On Cosmopolitanism and Forgiveness*, trans. Mark Dooley and Michael Hughes (London: Routledge, 1997); the aforementioned, Eliade, *The Sacred and the Profane*; Gayatri Chakravorty Spivak, *A Critique of Postcolonial Reason: Toward a History of the Vanishing Present* (Cambridge, MA: Harvard University Press, 1999); Homi K. Bhabha, *The Location of Culture* (London: Routledge, 2004).

Chapter 1

Indigenous Insights

FOUNDATIONS

In the context of North America, perhaps no assertion is as demanding of an apologetic riposte as Vine Deloria Jr.'s conviction that a proper religion needs a land of its own.¹ In the common Christian imaginary, this is nonsensical. Land, after all, is the cause of Middle Eastern tensions. Land issues underlay the not-so-civil wars of Ireland, the former Yugoslavia, etc., not to mention the expansive predilections of Nazi Germany. Land seems to be the cause of human problems, not the source of human solace, or so goes the Western mantra, that imagines land to be secular by nature, while time is fundamentally sacred in contrast. After all, we might assert, is not the eternal a category derived from time? And doesn't our religion demand a turn from material preoccupations to spiritual possessions that look to the *eschaton* as the locus for reframing this vale of tears? Well, perhaps this latter might incite an honest appraisal of the state of affairs in the Christian West.

It is not accidental that the Christian church has made use of the term *loci* to articulate a "fields" of study. *Loci*, of course, means places, and its theological deployment is parasitic on the Latin phrase *loci communes* which relates to the Greek philosophical strategy for memory. The function of *loci communes* (common places) was to allow the interested learner to associate important points to be memorized with places commonly frequented by crowds.² The ancient Greeks understood well the potency of place, which can be associated with a concept. Place mattered in the ancient mind, and it is a function of modern forgetfulness to forgo place in favor of time. This turn to time is of a piece with the Enlightenment, and yet modern Christians who want to redeploy the role of place in our imaginary can only do so at the cost of an honest appraisal of our propensity to isolate space's utility as a backdrop for mission.³ It is precisely this propensity that most annoys traditionalists from Indigenous religious traditions.⁴ Vine Deloria Jr. notes that Christians have inhabited a religious worldview growing out of a most ancient religion that was founded upon the promise of land. Abram's conversion to Abraham was consequent upon the promise that he and his clan would be given a land from which a people would erupt who would bless all the nations of the world. This people needed a land, a place to call home. This demand for place, then, is profoundly religious in nature. Yet Israel's relationship with its place became and remains problematic at so many levels. What comes of the religion in times of dispersion? What happens when Assyria, when Babylon, when Rome, when the Ottoman and the British empires lay claim on this land? A place to call our own becomes a moving target. Deloria makes the case that Christianity replaces "a promised land" with "heaven" to the end that end time preoccupations eclipse attention to land, place, and space.⁵ The continually contested relationship with the land is permanently resolved by a Christian turn to an eternal homeland called heaven. Here on the earth's land we are strangers and aliens (1 Pt. 2:11). We have no need of any particular place, any particular space, any particular land. Or so we say. But Deloria underscores that this prejudice fuels the Western phenomenon of making our religion a commodity for export.⁶ If we do not need any land, we can happily inhabit every land. Religion that doesn't need any particular land has now been given the condition for the possibility of imperialism. If my religion is not restricted to any particular place, it can exist quite readily in every place. This is Deloria's diagnosis of Christianity, and it most surely demands, as noted above, an apologetic riposte in both senses of the word apology. In the first sense, some of the comportments that have shaped Christian thought, praxis, and policy are most certainly in need of apology as repentance.⁷ Yet another kind of apology is needed. It is my firm conviction that Deloria's description of Christian convictions that remain unexamined also invites us both to own and to reframe what lay at the heart of Christianity: mission as foundational to Christian identity even while the primal category of mission speaks to our contested relationship with land. It is not accidental, in my estimation that missionaries speak of the mission *field*. In fact, this points to what we might imagine as a diagnosis of denial. In other words, Deloria articulates precisely the problematic for Christianity on the wane in the west and a warning for Christianity on the rise in the south: we need an honest appraisal of our relationship to land, place, and space precisely because the notion of mission that is in our DNA—and so undeniable—has regularly demonstrated both profound possibility and peril that it simply must be thought through with some care. A theological assessment of place attends to this, but with the *proviso* that Christianity has a profound need: an interlocutor that can honestly enable it to reassess its "mission" in a mode faithful to the gospel as the good news. Sadly, too many (certainly not all) missions have left far too little good in their wake. This legacy is especially evident in the Americas where the history of residential and boarding schools simply indicts churches of their collusion with an empire that demonstrated that it knows all too well the benefits accrued when empires "grab" land. This collusion came at the price of denying both our own dependency on land, space, and place and their power to reconstrue our relationship with the material. In what follows I purport a modest proposal; I want to engage the insights of Indigenous voices to the end that Christian dependence—and denial of that dependence—on land, place, and space is brought into relief to the end that a recognition and reconstrual of our relationship to place (as a broader catch term for the three) is renewed.

We turn, now, to the insights of interlocutors who can help those in the once Christian west to rethink our relationship to land, place, and space. It is noted, from this outset, that I use these words "lands, place, and space" as coreferents with increasing degrees of indeterminacy. Space stands in contrast to and in concert with time as a primordial mode of experience. Place locates more clearly the occasion of my experience of space. Land cannot be thought apart from soil, rock, and the geographical *topoi* that tell the tale of where my feet stand. It is to be noted that whereas many Western thinkers begin with time, Indigenous thinkers begin with the land. We turn now to them, so that we can learn something of what we purport to know by being reminded of what we have forgotten.

LAND, PLACE, AND SPACE

Perhaps no thinker has so clearly challenged Christianity's seeming indifference to land, place, and space as Vine Deloria Jr. With humor, insight, and considerable skill he has problematized many aspects of the Christian faith that we take for granted. Indeed, many of the problematic presuppositions he lists have served Christianity well in its colonizing phases of expansion and the accompanying period of modernity that has lived off the fats of this time. These very same characteristics, however, are indicted by Indigenous insights that carve apart a religious worldview in a postmodern era. As noted above, among the many challenges that Deloria poses to Christian thinkers perhaps the most important is his articulation of the manner in which Christianity has lost touch with the land. At the heart of this mis-placed religious sensibility is Christianity's inherited displacement of the theme of the promised land. Insofar as Christianity, more so than Judaism, has lost sight of the role of a particular place in according religious sensibilities, it has of necessity turned to history to locate its identity. Place becomes a backdrop for stories, in place of a locus wherein the believer encounters spiritual realities. By simple way of comparison, one can consider the importance of location for Aboriginal Australians, who see in the local topography traces of the primordial beings who in Dreamtime cause (note the intentional present tense) extents to be.[8] Creation in the Christian tradition, by contrast, has historically been located in a distant past, and theology is a recollection of this creation, the subsequent fall, and God's reclamation of sinners in Christ (at least in Christian versions of the same).[9] Deloria queries this and does so in a fashion thoroughly consistent with a worldview that begins with place. If, he asks, we begin theology where we are, and where we are speaks to religious truths, then those truths are going to reflect this location. There is, following from this, no place for a universal religion. Religion rooted in place is going to be of necessity local. Christianity's turn to history, necessitated by an inherited dis-placement, gives Christians an inordinate interest in time in service of the universal. A host of complications follow from this: buildings replace nature as the proper place for worship; preaching and teaching replace ritual as the religious center, to the effect that head takes precedence over heart and hands; a kind of utilitarian view of creation soon obtains to the end that the human as master of creation attains a kind of God-like status that upends our relationship with the environment: the list goes on. Little good for First Nations will come from a religious dialogue with Christianity, in Deloria's estimation. A few Indigenous peoples agree with this assessment, but not all.

George "Tink" Tinker, by his own admission, owes much to Deloria. Yet he holds forth the importance of a dialogue in a manner that seems to be missing in Deloria. Tinker finds his point of orientation, like Deloria, in the importance of place for thinking theologically. He notes, as well, that there are four key points of disagreement between Indigenous sensibilities and mainstream Christian thought: the importance of space, the role of land, the place of community, and the significance of creation.[10] Unlike Deloria, however, Tinker seems to indicate that there are resources within Christianity for reclaiming some of these important themes for Christians. In particular, he notes the utility of the first article of the creed for a re-reading of Christianity that might invite the Christian to consider that the Reign of God is more a where than a when concept.[11] In so doing, however, he notes that a turn to the first article counters much Christian discourse.[12] He especially notes that this is a path that runs counter to the Lutheran (and Reformed) practice of preaching law and gospel. He is especially suspicious of Lutheranism, where the law is understood to be an expression of God's demand of humans in light of their sinfulness. The law pricks consciences to the end that they despair of their own ability and are then prepared to hear the good news of the gospel: God accepts sinners unconditionally. Tinker suggests that Lutheranism does not work for Indigenous peoples.[13] This topic will be further discussed in the second chapter. Suffice to say at this point that if Lutheranism is to have any utility in North America, it can only be by the grace of a chastening that helps Lutherans and Lutheranism to rethink its relationship to land, place, and time. How might theological insights from First Nations help on this front?

Deloria et al. speak continually of the need to reclaim land as a central value.[14] It strikes me that this will require the deployment of two strategies that will focus and prioritize how we think about land, place, and space in what follows. The first will require us to think about this triad in terms of specificity. The second will invite us to think about land in terms of agency. On both accounts, Christians have much to learn from Indigenous thinkers. I begin with the former.

Basil Johnston has spoken of the one who created the land, the one called Kitchi-Manitou in Ojibway. The very name Kitchi-Manitou is difficult to translate. He has noted that the Manitou, although often rendered "spirit" means so much more.[15] Manitou can refer to life force, being, God, spirit, anima, force, etc. Kitchi qualifies Manitou as especially great in this instance of its discussion. So, then, Kitchi-Manitou is a spiritual energy, or even presence, that is so great that it cannot be adequately described, and certainly not circumscribed. Johnston speaks of the manner in which Kitchi-Manitou is everywhere. Yet he also notes that most Indigenous tellings of this presence point to its especial concentration in certain locales. While God is everywhere, God is also profoundly present in certain places, and so humans visit particular places in times of trial and moments in which special guidance or direction is needed.

In a fashion, what Johnston has to say to us about Kitchi-Manitou invites us to think more specifically about land, place, and space in a different manner. Perhaps one could compare this way of thinking about God to how we experience the smoke from a fire. From a distance we are aware of a fire by its smoke. We see it from a distance, as one element in the vista that we observe. As we get closer to a fire, the smoke becomes more prominent; now we can smell the smoke as well as see it. As we get closer still, we begin to taste the smoke, and its presence on our sensual table becomes more prominent. Finally, if it is a forest fire, when we are in the midst of it, it is all-consuming. In a fashion, this way of imaging Kitchi-Manitou under the tutelage of smoke might also serve as a trope for rethinking how we talk about space, place, and land. Space serves as a more general cipher of what is not time, yet as such remains at a distance from our sensual knowing. Place becomes a bit more specific and allows us to identify the category of space with a higher degree of specificity. Space becomes place when it is identified with a narrative of the people.[16] Yet a still higher degree of specificity becomes possible when we think about land. We cannot think land without a turn to the senses: just as we move from seeing to smelling to tasting smoke the closer we get to a fire, so we cannot think about land in the abstract. Land only is accessible by means of memory of particular places, where our feet have trod, where our knees have been scraped, watering holes where we swam as children, particular loci that make up the stories of our existence at an existential level.[17] In fact, the more intentionally we think about land, the less land becomes a backdrop for our storied existence and becomes instead a character in the story. We are invited to imagine the agency of land.

North American First Nations will speak often of the land as their mother. "Mother Earth" is not unknown in other circles as well. Perhaps the First Nations of the Americas take this a bit more seriously than occidental thinkers. This tendency to take land more seriously is nested in a series of stories about creation, and about the nature of the land we live in. In many of these stories animals hold councils regarding the state of affairs of the humans, the last of Kitchi-Manitou's creation.[18] Yet not only animals take on human-like characteristics. The wind, the sea, even mountains have human characteristics—such as mood in Ojibway thought.[19] For the Inuit, to cite another example, the sky itself is associated with reason and is accorded a person-like status in light of its spiritual powers.[20] The world is thick with spiritual forces that know, will, and decide. The mother of all these forces is the land. The land births us and so can be imagined as a character in the story that is our existence. It is important to remember that the land is not our Creator, but our mother. The land belongs to Kitchi-Manitou.[21] The land is not worshipped but devoutly respected and honored as a mother. It is this fundamental insight that radically reframes the sordid story of land misappropriation of lands by Europeans. The First Nations of the Americas really had a different understanding of the role of the treaty with respect to land "ownership."[22] How can you "own" your Mother?[23] The land is not something that can be bought and sold, so much as someone who is to be honored, respected, and valued as a member of the family. The land is our relative, but not just any relative. For most Indigenous thought, the land is a living repository of the narratives that explain, explore, and express spirituality. This is what lay behind Deloria's assertion that the validity of a religion is contingent upon its relationship with land. A landless religion, in his estimation, is really no religion at all.[24] Where does that leave Christianity?

Christianity's history on the land called the Americas is profoundly sad, disturbing, and troubling. Our collusion with the expansion of empire seems to be too often blind and deaf to a fundamental insight: "empire never seems to learn that brutal expansion has no future."[25] Christianity has been taken in by the colonial fiction that unchecked growth is a mark of health, even while medical practitioners call the same cancer. Insofar as Christianity imbibes at the well of manifest destiny, it allows itself to be defined by the fiction that its landless character gives is unparalleled entrée into all nations, every people, and each place. Christianity's landless character, according to Deloria, is at the heart of its colonizing propensity. I think that Deloria is on to something here, insofar as he identifies our inability to think doxologically about land, place, and space with our susceptibility to manipulation by empire. Moreover, this refusal to think through place's agency is at odds with Scriptural witness that speaks of creation's groaning, hills that praise, and stars that sing. Our need to reimagine place in this way is at the heart of a revitalization of Christianity in a chastened, but for that reason, more authentic form.

Deloria is not very hopeful about the future of Christianity. Yet he holds forth the possibility that if a religion is adaptable to its locale in the state of diaspora there is a possibility for a healthy immigration.[26] Clearly, much work is needed. Brueggemann has noted that the United States sees itself as the new Israel, when really it is more like Babylon.[27] This observation certainly serves to chasten North American self-understandings. Yet beyond this, Christians need to imagine the presence of Christianity in the Americas under the discipline of the image of the immigrant. Just as all immigrants experience their own morphing in their new locale, so too, Christianity is bound to be refashioned if it lives authentically in relationship with its new land. The First Nations of the Americas alone can school us on what it is that we need to learn from the land. We turn now to consider some of their further insights.

STARTING WITH WE: DISSENT AS GIFT

The Cree theologian Ray Aldred describes the difference between First Nations culture and the dominant culture in North America by asserting, "We start with we."[28] This way of being and thinking is not, of course, unique to the First Nations of the Americas. In fact, this way of thinking has been the primary way of being for most of the millennia of human history. The turn to the subject is a marker of modernity and distinguishes the modern from the premodern worldview. Moreover, the press to embracing alterity in so-called postmodern paradigms speaks to the perduring character of that emphasis, and in fact, underscores that even in the peak of modernity, the notion of community was never really lost, but rather muted.[29] That being said, in the context of the Americas, the Indigenous emphasis on we is not inconsequential as an invitation, or better yet, a call for Christians to reframe their commitment to the individual as the starting point in theological discourse. Precisely this could be construed as a recollection of the gift of being in Christ, given anew in the Americas by the First Nations. In what follows I explore the contours of that recollection by first underscoring the turn to the community as the starting point, then pointing to the manner in which community is read in a far more expansive mode than that typical for contemporary North American

Christians, and finally by noting the underlying embrace of difference in both of these.

At one level, the grounding of Indigenous epistemology in the "we" is simply a function of the demand of the land. Living off the buffalo, or living in the harsh climate of the Arctic, to cite two examples, underscore the need for communal cooperation for subsistence. Yet, it is important to note from the outset that First Nation's notion of community does not preclude the importance of the individual. Rupert Ross, in discussing the distinction between Indigenous and European cultures, discovers that a radical freedom was and is permitted to individuals in Indigenous traditions, yet with the expectation that experience will point people to the community of their own free will.[30] By the grace of the interaction of the individual and the community, human life flourishes and this flourishing points in two directions: language and story.

As noted above, Thomas King asserts that in an Indigenous framework, "stories are all that we are."[31] Stories, as such, both explain and shape life in community. Moreover, in so doing, they resist the dogmatism that sometimes accompanies a Christian reduction of our fundamental stories into discrete and often-times divorced propositions. Stories articulate the relationships between life, land, and the Creator. The community is the repository of these stories, rather than books. In a sense, the shift from an oral to a written culture remains a significant paradigm shift for the First Nations of the Americas. Storytelling presumes that certain people have both the gift of remembering and imparting the right story at the right time. It is not to be presumed that anyone can, at any time, go to some communal index wherein she finds the right story to answer the pressing problem or escape the long winter night. Storytelling is a gift given to the community, rather than the individual. This gift is, of course, nested in the gift of language. Indigenous thinkers across the Americas recognize that the loss of language is one of the most pressing problems. I recall visiting two Cree friends who explained the significance of language for their worldview. In a fashion reminiscent for anyone who does translation work, one noted that there are significant Cree concepts that can only be hinted at in translation. The other, however, went further to say that he experienced some of his fellow band members differently in English. Their being shifted when they spoke English and the other attributed that shift to English being a language of business and law on the reserve. All of this reflects, of course, the fact that language comes to us from community and reflects our mode of being as communal. As soon as we speak, we participate in community because the very act of speaking betrays our dependence on community. Insofar as language itself reflects that community it transmits something of the communal character of being. But what is the nature of Indigenous communities?

Of course, it is impossible to speak monolithically of "the" character of the Indigenous community in the Americas, especially in light of the above assertion that language expresses and shapes that culture and the number of Indigenous languages in the Americas is staggering. However, there are some points of overlap. Especially significant is the manner in which the First Nations discourse about community reflects a much broader notion of *who* is to be counted in the community. We see this in two directions. On the one hand, community includes all to whom Mother Earth gives birth, which is to say, all created beings. On the other, community includes not only those born but the not yet born and the already dead. As for the first point, Indigenous hunters generally include in the act of killing an animal a word of apology and thanksgiving to the animal killed for the good of the community. This is because animals are seen to be our kin.[32] Moreover, relatives are not simply restricted to animals in some Indigenous cultures. Certain communities in North America make extensive use of sweat lodges, in which water is poured over hot rocks. The rocks are said to speak to us in the sound that accompanies this. The significance of this is only evident when one ponders that rocks are deemed to be grandfathers, that is, the oldest living beings on the planets.[33] The Indigenous ritual of listening to the rocks speak bespeaks a much richer notion of community than one common to Christians, even though the Christian scriptures describe the earth groaning, mountains bearing witness, etc.[34] Yet beyond this broader understanding of community, which draws in the creation, a common practice in the Indigenous communities in which I have lived includes asking the question, "How will our decisions today impact the next seven generations?" Taiaike Alfred speaks of our need to listen to the grandfathers yet to come.[35] In sum, the notion of community embraced herein is one that is broader and richer than that often experienced by the Western individual. Perhaps this is what makes people sometimes wistfully pine for a simpler life, which they associate with Indigenous sensibilities. Yet, on another level, this life is anything but simple, insofar as it presumes that being together means living with difference.

In writing about the life of the famed Plains Cree Chief Big Bear, Rudy Wiebe notes that Big Bear succeeded as an exemplary leader because he understood that to be a chief was to be a servant.[36] This theme is echoed in Alfred's assertion that the only real power available to leaders in traditional Indigenous communities is the power to persuade.[37] Moreover, he notes the manner in which traditional Indigenous communities had dissipated patterns of leadership: different people could be identified as leaders across a variety of communal activities that include hunting, making war and treaty, religious rituals, and healing. The notion that there should be one figurehead as chief along with a council was a requirement of colonial powers rather than a fact of native governance.[38]

Diversity seems to be written into the script of the First Nations. Moreover, it is interesting to note that even foundational stories, such as creation myths, are not understood to be universal.[39] Indeed, insofar as diversity is written into creation it is seen to be a profound and important gift. Dissent and the possibility of a radical freedom is common to Indigenous worldviews.[40] The presumption, again, is that by allowing people to follow their own path, they will be led to learning from God who uses land as well as the elders to teach people to live in a good way. We find that the land returns as an important character in the narrative of human life. Yet the land, no less than the narrower human community, still has lessons to teach us insofar as we sometimes stray from the good way. What do we learn from Indigenous relationship to the land about human sin, frailty, and evil?

ORIGINAL SANCTITY, ORIGINAL BALANCE

One of the places where the Christian tradition most stands in contrast to the thought of many Indigenous insights and religious worldviews revolves around sin. Although one cannot simply assert an undifferentiated articulation of an Indigenous doctrine of sin—since doctrine is really a Christian category and functions as a particular practice of the Christian religion—one can still discern enough commonality across a host of Indigenous stories that allow one to distinguish a fundamental motif that stands in stark contrast to most articulations of sin in the Christian tradition. One could summarize it with the term "original sanctity" in the place of "original sin."[41] Or, as the Ojibway elder and scholar Basil Johnston articulates, humans are born with an innate goodness.[42] Of course, this represents a fundamentally different starting point for thinking through a theological anthropology. Many Christian scholars would, at first glance, simply label this as naïve. We will revisit this observation after further unpacking some of the insights garnered from beginning with original sanctity.

An Indigenous understanding of human existence is sometimes articulated using the vision of the circle. Circles recur consistently in stories, teachings, architecture, and social construction in the many nations of the Americas. Time itself is primarily understood under the category of the circle rather than under the paradigm of progress.[43] Of course, in both the Jewish and Christian tradition, a circular notion of time is profoundly important. After all, in Christian churches today still we sing, "Jesus Christ is risen today" each Easter morning. Yet without any doubt, this view was increasingly marginalized in that epochal break called the Enlightenment. The notion of a time as a trajectory in motion toward a fulfillment became the principal means by which we understood life. Native thinkers problematize this view for us, not by first querying our notion of time, but by problematizing our explanation of evil.

There is no fall narrative in Indigenous religious worldviews. Consequently, there is no Eden. No fall; no Eden. What does this do to the broader religious imagination? What if the end or purpose of religion is no longer an after-life that recalls an Edenic beginning? Where does this lead us? Is this a hopelessly naïve understanding of human life? It should be underscored from the outset that the absence of a narrative of a fall cannot be equated to a willful blindness to the human experience of brokenness. No, rather it is the case that human brokenness is about human disequilibrium that is preventable. Humans are born whole and die whole by walking in a good way, following appropriate rituals and the guidance of the Creator.[44]

Rupert Ross has noted that the primary trope for understanding the brokenness of human life is one of illness or misunderstanding rather than ill will. Consequently, the remedies for this brokenness are healing and teaching.[45] There was no such thing as incarceration in Indigenous imaginaries; banishment was an extreme response to human brokenness and rarely evoked.[46] Ross also notes that it is a linear worldview that allows us to dispose of things and people.[47] If life is a trajectory to a static point, then casting aside what weighs one down seems sound. I would argue that this trope is the condition for the possibility of a culture of incarceration wherein the prison becomes a cipher for banishment.[48] Yet, if our principal experience of life is not one of a journey to a distant destination, but living in a circular fashion in the land given to us, then there is no leaving behind. We always come back to what we left behind. Historically, the church has affirmed the truth of this with the church season of Lent. Every year we return to what we left behind as a perduring task. In contrast to this practice, which has *some* resonance with an Indigenous perspective, the modern nation-state—especially insofar as it imagines itself to have a manifest destiny—acts in a fashion that allows us to leave behind whatever weighs us down in order to achieve that *telos* so far removed from now. In contrast, First Nations assert that we will finally be where we are, and everything we leave behind we simply re-encounter. The solution to the problems of brokenness revolves around rituals that restore harmony rather than purify an original stain. Randy Woodley describes this in considering the ancient Cherokee cementation ceremony:

> The basic components of the ceremony included a fire and prayers that were spoken by the holy person. Then the families and friends on each side of the riff would face each other with the lead person (those with whom the division originated) at the head of the line. Each would give an account of the offense. Then the person would go to the fire to pray for the strength to forgive. The two would then strip naked and exchange clothes. Following this action they spoke

words of forgiveness and vowed never to bring the issue up again. The pipe was passed back and forth down the line for everyone to smoke. Finally, gifts were exchanged and a feast was prepared by both parties of the whole community. The result was both ceremonial and practical.[49]

What this represents is the wisdom of communities that recognize that you cannot leave behind your enemies. The reality of living with those who exacerbate us demands the ritual of "healing the riff" under the presumption that there is a misunderstanding, or illness, that requires repairing a breach of some kind. Traditional Native American accounts of what Christians call "sin" presume that there is no original sin behind particular instances of sin. Consequently, there is no need to repair the breach of original sin by way of baptism, or rebirth. Rather, specific responses to particular infractions of communal life are advanced. The vision that guides such responses to brokenness is one of a primary balance between humans, God, and creation. This vision evokes a posture of awe and wonder.[50] Sin is primarily understood in relationship to our day-to-day interactions with one another and our living in balance with creation and the Creator.[51]

What is fundamentally different about this vision is that it denies us the comfort of imagining a primal place of human flourishing. At a fundamental level, the image of Eden controls far more of Christian discourse than we acknowledge. At a popular level in Christian thought, this Edenic vision is transposed into the image of a distant heaven wherein we will be able to "leave behind" the problems of sin and sinners. Such a rapture is an evasion of the human situation and its consequent responsibility, in the Indigenous imagination. What might this possibly mean for a Christian wishing to articulate a renewed appreciation of land, place, and space?

From the outset, my conviction is one in which jettisoning my tradition's teaching on sin and evil would simply replicate an ethic of "leaving behind." What needs to happen, instead, is a return to what the Christian church has said about sin and redemption, yet with a new appreciation for inhabiting the land, place, and space given to us. Randy Woodley is an Indigenous theologian who does precisely that in the following:

> I am not convinced that the Eden myth explains what Euro-western theologian call "human depravity" as much as it explains what many Indigenous people understand as disequilibrium.[52]

Woodley succeeds in exemplifying the value of comparative theology. He considers another religious worldview, and then returns to Christian theology with a fresh perspective, one that many would deem to be more faithful to the Christian scriptures. After all, Jewish theologians read the same Genesis texts and do not have the same notion of original sin that has been articulated in the Christian tradition. Moreover, their articulation of original sin has not fallen captive to certain themes in modernity that have enticed a paradisiacal vision of reality. We have much to learn from the First Nations of the Americas, especially insofar as they have lived in this place without the dangerous luxury of imagining it either as an Eden or as a stopping point on the way to Eden. Moreover, it is important to note that Indigenous thinkers are not unaware of evil and its irrational character. Many in the part of the continent in which I live point to the myth of the Weendigo as a story that locates the human reality of greed as the source of much disequilibrium. The Weendigo is a monster (in some versions originally a human who has taken the drastic act of practicing cannibalism[53]) that feeds upon human flesh. This feeding, however, is such that it does not sate hunger, but further feeds it. Hunger itself is never abated by such feeding. Greed is never sated. Basil Johnston, in discussing this mythological creature suggests the following:

> Even though a Weendigo is a mythical figure, it represents real human cupidity. However, as time went by, more and more learned people declared that such monsters were a product of superstitious minds and imaginations.
>
> As a result, the Weendigoes were driven from their place in Anishinaube traditions and culture and ostracized by disbelief and skepticism. . . . Actually, the Weendigoes did not die out or disappear; they have only been assimilated and reincarnated as corporations, conglomerates and multinationals.[54]

By understanding that the place we are in is the place where we will ever be, Johnston puts to rest the notion of the place we live as being a resource for consumption in our press to some Edenic *telos* that funds the dangerous comportment of greed. Harmony is the Indigenous answer to the question of greed, and harmony is ever understood in relationship not only to other people and the Creator but also to this place some called Turtle Island, a land marked aboriginally by boundaries rather than borders.

PERMEABLE BOUNDARIES, PERMEABLE PEOPLE

Thomas King, with characteristic clarity, asserts that borders don't mean much to most native people.[55] This must not be construed under the canons of a liberal paradigm that seeks a utopian community of humankind, in which everyone just loves one another and agrees to get along. Native communities in North America, not unlike peoples the world over, generally had some sense of where they belonged and recognized that crossing their boundaries into the territory of another was not to be done without proper protocol. Yet something fundamental changes when the beginning point for this occurs under a different understanding of the theme of "belonging." The people belong to the land; the land does not belong to the people. And the land is bigger than my instance of belonging to it. Fundamentally, our relationship to a place relates us to all place differently. This difference allows for the possibility of re-construing our notion of border to the end that we understand them as permeable boundaries negotiable by the wax and wane of the hunt, our relationships with our neighbors and our relationship with our Creator. This latter is fundamental.

The Great Spirit creates. This is a notion shared between adherents of Christianity and traditionalists in First Nations. Yet, as noted above, something fundamentally different accrues in an Indigenous portrayal of creation. Creation stories are not finally about the human alone, but about the human in community with the Creator, and all created realities. Humans are not a species above other species in the order of creation.[56] Two truths follow from this. First, it presumes a refusal of an absolute border reframing humanity's relationship vis à vis both creation and the Creator, as well as that within humanity itself. We consider each in turn.

Vine Deloria makes the case that in tribal religions, the distinction between the human and the animal is such that one can become the other and vice versa.[57] Myths and stories often portray talking creatures that betray characteristics that occidental thinkers would typically restrict to *homo sapiens*. Indeed, many versions of Indigenous spirituality include some version of a vision quest in which humans seek wisdom from the manitous that come via—or as—an animal. The spiritual world and the animal world are not cut off from one another anymore than the animal world from the human world. Spirit, humanity, and creation are intertwined. Nowhere is this so clearly seen as in the common use of the Trickster character in native myths.

Trickster is a boundary character who crosses borders in many ways.[58] Sometimes taking the form of a human, sometimes taking the form of an animal, Trickster morphs along with the stories as need be. But it would be a mistake to discredit this shift because it is "just a story." And while King proclaims that "stories are all we have,"[59] it also seems that stories are all we are. Stories constitute us in community by relating us to the world around us and to the God who creates us in and as this world. The Trickster character is of a piece with this fundamental element of storytelling; indeed, in some instances, the storyteller is the Trickster. Trickster mirrors the human condition in both noble and ignoble ways. Trickster hints at our rich relationship with the divine, crossing boundaries, shifting shapes, stretching across time, and yielding fundamental insights. Some Indigenous people identify Jesus with the Trickster character.[60]

The Trickster character is not typically without vice. He mirrors human foolishness from time to time, as well as our human propensity to be self-absorbed.[61] It is important to underscore the relationship between the Trickster character and story. Trickster is not a dogmatic category, in the same sense that some Christians would understand Christology, for instance. The role of Trickster is fluid, nuanced, and evocative. By mirroring, and sometimes mocking, human characteristics we are invited to see both our foibles and our fortitude. We are able to see both our spiritual nature and our profound attachment to the land and its stories. We are not a species apart, but a species only by being a part of the telling of a place. To know a place is to know its stories, and the storied character of Indigenous identity is replete with shift. Humans can become indistinguishable from animals in some instances, and manitous can become indistinguishable from humans in others. Yet these shifting boundaries, or limits, are not the sole constitution of our existence. There is also a core. The peripheral sites of permeability and wound do not preclude a kind of center to human existence.[62] In the same manner—as noted above with respect to Kitze Manitou who is everywhere yet concentrated in certain places—the human shifts across boundaries yet has a kind of a constituted and constituting core. This brings us to consider what this core looks like and the contours of its existence.

Many Indigenous peoples in North America have been nomadic, or semi-nomadic. This pattern of living served them well for the many generations that preceded contact. Tragically, settlers interpreted this as evidence that these people of the land were not "civilized" since the occidental construal of "civilization" presumed the sharply defined borders of the emerging notion of the nation-state. To be Indigenous in the Americas was to be on the move in some fashion or another, and this allowed for a flexibility in both social roles and a construal of humankind's relationship with the earth.

Perhaps one of the most surprising of these construals is the tradition of the berdache in certain parts of Turtle Island.[63] The berdache were people who some might consider sexually indeterminate: sometimes playing the role of male, sometimes female.[64] Such people were not considered to be abnormal, but a particular part of the normality of the community that is diverse. The berdache tradition points beyond the problem of sexual politics to the expectation that, at some level, communal life took account of the shifting shape of roles period. Lee Maracle notes that Raven—representing the Creator—shapes us for transformation.[65] Humans who live on the land know that malleability—within the constraints of the stories that constitute our existence—is virtuous. For this reason, there is a mandate to find the freedom that fits the context of our inhabitation.[66] This is not a mindless, nor a formless, freedom, but rather a freedom shaped by the place in which we find ourselves and always attentive of the need to live with some balance:

"Finally, we people who are 'walking earth' should face the fact that we cannot continue on these destructive paths without hurting ourselves and our future generations. We are all truly related."[67] This is not an absolute freedom, but a freedom prescribed by the place of our being and ordered toward the good of all beings. Rigidity does not describe the land which gives us birth, and so we—like our Mother—are constituted as people who move; across boundaries, across roles, and across traditions, yet ever respectful of those who have gone before us (because they are with us), those who will come after us (because we will be with them), and the land (because the Creator has made us to be one with our Mother). Permeability and flexibility are marks of people who live in a good way on the land attentive to the place we have been given. What might this mean for followers of the one we call the Way, the Truth, and the Life?

TAKING PLACE SERIOUSLY

Brazilian theologian Vitor Westhelle has spoken of the church as a hybrid place.[68] The church, as it is faithful to the gospel, lives at the margins where the so-called distinction between the sacred and secular is blurred. In fulfilling this task the church becomes an eschatological community. Eschatological here is re-imagined under the category of space, rather than time.[69] This is a helpful notion for reframing how we think about space, place, and land. In sum, Westhelle helps us to rethink not only our notion of church but also our construal of place. In bringing eschatology and place together, he allows us to reimagine their interrelationship. Consequently, I posit the notion that place can be construed kairotically, a theme developed more fulsomely in the fourth and fifth chapters.

The term *kairos*, like the word *eschatos*, is predominantly aligned with notions of time, and properly so. Greek lexicons underscore how "*kairos*" is a welcoming time, or the right and favorable time.[70] *Kairos* is also identified as a "chief eschatological term." Insofar as we are able to construe eschatology in relationship to space in addition to time, we are then able to imagine—analogously—that such a space shares the distinction that we know to exist between *chronos* and *kairos*. *Chronos* as ordinary, regular, cyclical time is different from *kairos* as that extraordinary experience of time, wherein time is fulfilled. In a similar fashion, we can imagine—as indicated in Basil Johnston's thoughts about the presence of Kitchi-Manitou—that certain places are extraordinary.[71] The Creator is, like the fog, present everywhere, but that presence is especially potent at certain sites, as well as at certain times since time and space finally cannot be ripped apart from one another. In the chapters that follow, we will explore the conditions under which place becomes *kairotic*, and so allows us the possibility of taking place seriously. In so doing, we will put some of the insights garnered from Indigenous sources above, in conversation with two seminal thinkers in the Christian tradition: Martin Luther and Friedrich Schleiermacher. Luther, read in dialogue with various voices will press us to reframe our understanding of space, place, and land. He invites us to imagine a kenotic Creator whose presence gifts us with natural and civil laws aiming at cosmic harmony in service of justice and mercy.

Schleiermacher then allows us to consider how this experience of the place under the category of the *kairos* will allow us to explore the ways in which place might be thought under the rubric of "harmony." *Kairotic* space is harmonious and so allows the suspension of zero-sum thinking that frames much of our apprehensions of land, place, and space. In due course, these two insights will provide us with resources for considering the poetics of space, the very condition for the possibility of reframing Christianity's contested relationship to space, place, and land. Moreover, as we think concretely about the land we inhabit, and its increasingly pluralistic character, we will recognize places and moments ascending as we meet our neighbors, who in good Samaritan fashion call us out of ourselves so that we might be who are.

As we being to take place seriously we will, bit by bit, take up Vine Deloria Jr.'s challenge—an especially pertinent task in light of the manner in which the church has largely been party to colonial designs on space, place, and land. We turn now to consider Luther in conversation with Indigenous insights.

NOTES

1. Deloria, *Custer Died for Your Sins*, 179, 180.
2. See Richard Sorabji, *Aristotle on Memory*, 2nd ed. (Chicago: University of Chicago Press, 2004), 22–26.
3. See Mk. 16:15. "Go into all the world and proclaim the good news to the whole creation" (NRSV).
4. Vine Deloria Jr. *God Is Red: A Native View of Religion* (Golden, CO: Fulcrum Pub., 2003), 65.
5. Ibid., 142, 72.
6. Deloria, *Custer Died for Your Sins*, 109.
7. The Canadian government, to cite one example, apologized for its treatment of First Nations on June 11, 2008. "Government Apologies for Residential Schools in 2008," CBC last updated June 25, 2018, https://www.cbc.ca/archives/government-apologizes-for-residential-schools-in-2008-1.4666041. Deloria queries a Christian disposition that continues still to see the First Nations of the Americas as a mission field. Cf, *Custer Died for Your Sins*, 112.

8. See Robin Koning, "Walking the Land: Inculturation and Footprints in the Western Desert of Australia," *Toronto Journal of Theology* 21, no. 1 (Spring 2005): 97.

9. Deloria sees this narrowing of the category of creation to questions of origins to be a function of the displacement of a promised land with heaven in Christian thought. *God Is Red*, 142.

10. Tinker, *American Indian Liberation*, 7.

11. Ibid., 52.

12. Ibid., 42.

13. Ibid., 90.

14. Deloria, *God Is Red*, 246.

15. Johnston, *The Manitous*, 2.

16. Walter Brueggemann, *The Land: Place as Gift, Promise, and Challenge in Biblical Faith*, 2nd ed. (Minneapolis, MN: Fortress Press, 2002), 4.

17. See Bachelard, *The Poetics of Space*, 9. Mary (Joy) Philip, in speaking of human interaction, notes "It is a memory that makes present. When bodies come together, when one's skin touches another's skin, it leaves an imprint, not the visible mark of an unforgettable person, but an invisible and yet an unerasable mark, a presence." "Remembrance," in *Churrasco: A Theological Feast in Honor of Vítor Westhelle*, eds. Mary Philip, John Arthur Nunes, and Charles M. Collier (Eugen, OR: Pickwick, 2013), 99. Of course, what is true for a body is true for our interaction with the body of Mother Earth.

18. Basil Johnston, *Ojibway Heritage* (Toronto: McClelland and Stewart, 1976), 11–17.

19. Ibid., 33, 34.

20. Frédéric B. Laugrand and Jarich G. Oosten, *Inuit Shamanism and Christianity: Transitions and Transformations in the Twentieth Century* (Montreal and Kingston: McGill-Queen's University Press, 2010), 142, 143.

21. Basil Johnston, "The Wampum Belts Tells Us," in *Our Story: Aboriginal Voices on Canada's Past*, ed. Rudyard Griffiths (Toronto: Anchor Canada, 2004), 91.

22. See Rudy Wiebe, *Big Bear* (Toronto: Penguin Canada, 2008), 143. Cf also Harold Cardinal, "Okimaw Win and Post-colonial Nation-Building," in *Intersecting Voices: Critical Theologies in a Land of Diversity*, eds. Don Schweitzer and Derek Simon (Toronto: Novalis Press, 2004), 197.

23. A point made in conversation with Ray Aldred, a Cree theologian to whom I owe much.

24. Deloria, *Custer Died for Your Sins*, 179, 180.

25. Brueggeman, "Alien Witness: How God's People Challenge Empire," *The Christian Century* 124, no. 5 (March 6, 2007): 30.

26. Deloria, *God Is Red*, 292.

27. Brueggeman, "Alien Witness," 28.

28. Ray Aldred, "Freedom: A Cree Theologian's Account" (lecture, Waterloo Lutheran Seminary, Wilfrid Laurier University, November 12, 2012).

29. Schleiermacher, to cite one example, in his treatment of election makes the surprising assertion that God's act of election is primarily of humanity as a whole, and only derivatively applicable to individuals. See Friedrich Schleiermacher, *On The Doctrine*

of Election with Special Reference to the Aphorisms *of Dr. Bretschneider*, trans. Iain G. Nicol and Allen G. Jorgenson (Louisville: Westminster John Knox Press, 2011), 76.

30. Ross, *Dancing with a Ghost*, 14, 49, 75.
31. King, *The Truth About Stories*, 2.
32. Clara Sue Kidwell, Homer Noley, and George "Tink" Tinker, in *A Native American Theology* (Maryknoll: Orbis Press, 2001), 81.
33. Elder Jean Becker, Senior Advisor—Office of Aboriginal Initiatives, "Untitled" (lecture, Wilfrid Laurier University, Waterloo, Ontario February 2011).
34. See Ps. 19;:1–4; Ps. 68:1–4; Ps. 69:34; Ps. 89:5; Ps. 97:6; Ps. 114; Ps. 148; Rom. 8:18–23; 2 Cor. 5:17; Col. 1:23.
35. Taiaike Alfred, *Peace, Power and Righteousness: An Indigenous Manifesto*, 2nd ed. (Oxford: Oxford University Press, 2009), 20.
36. Wiebe, *Big Bear*, 33.
37. Alfred, *Peace, Power and Righteousness*, 20.
38. Ibid., 90. See also Ross, *Dancing with a Ghost*, 3.
39. Deloria, *God Is Red*, 87.
40. Ross, *Dancing with a* Ghost, 14.
41. Ibid., 193.
42. Johnston, in "Introduction" to *Dancing with a Ghost*, xiii.
43. Kidwell et al., *A Native American Theology*, 13.
44. Lisa A. Dellinger, "Sin—Ambiguity and Complexity and the Sin of Not Conforming," in *Coming Full Circle: Constructing Native Christian Theology*, eds. Steven Charleston and Elaine A. Robinson (Minneapolis: Fortress Press, 2015), 125.
45. Ross, *Dancing with a Ghost*, 71, 193.
46. Ibid., 154.
47. Ibid., 186.
48. Australia, of course, comes to mind.
49. Randy S. Woodley, *Shalom and the Community of Creation: An Indigenous Vision* (Grand Rapids, MI: William B. Eerdmans Pub. Co., 2012), 23.
50. Kidwell et al., *A Native American Theology*, 33.
51. Ibid., 118.
52. Woodley, *Shalom and the Community of Creation*, 68.
53. Johnston, *The Manitous*, 224, 227.
54. Ibid., 235.
55. King, *The Truth About Stories*, 102.
56. Tinker, *American Indian Liberation*, 40.
57. Deloria, *God Is Red*, 89.
58. Kidwell et al., *A Native American* Theology, 119.
59. King, *The Truth About Stories*, 2.
60. Kidwell et al., *A Native American Theology*, 122.
61. A delightful modern rendering of the Trickster character is offered by Drew Hayden Taylor in *Motorcycles and Sweetgrass: A Novel* (Toronto: Knopf, 2010).
62. See Mary (Joy) Philip, "The Space In Between Spaces: The Church as Prophetic Pest/Parasite," in *Being the Church in the Midst of Empire: Trinitarian*

Reflections, ed. Karen L. Bloomquist (Minneapolis, MN: Lutheran University Press, 2007), 91–106.

63. Gerald Hannon, "The Pink Indian," *Toronto Life,* September, 2011, 56–62.

64. Ibid., 57.

65. Lee Maracle, "Goodbye, Snaug," in *Our Story*, 205.

66. Ibid., 205. Achiel Peelman notes that "Many Native Christians often continue to cross the border between their Christian religion and their traditional spirituality, especially at the subjective or emotional level (personal healing, reconciliation, restoration of social relationships) and life-cycle decisions (rites of passage), even in communities where the churches have been present for generations." In "The Meeting of the Rivers: Being Native and Christian in Canada," *Toronto Journal of Theology* 21, no. 1 (Spring 2005): 18.

67. Woodley, *Shalom and the Community of Creation*, 86.

68. See Vitor Westhelle, "Liberation Theology: A Latitudinal Perspective," in *The Oxford Handbook of Eschatology*, ed. Jerry L. Walls (Oxford: Oxford University Press, 2008), 318.

69. See Westhelle, *Eschatology and Space*; Kathryn Tanner, "Eschatology and Ethics," in *The Oxford Handbook of Theological Ethics,* eds. Gilbert Meilaender and William Werpehowski (Oxford: Oxford University Press, 2005), 41–56; Allen G. Jorgenson, "Empire, Eschatology and Stolen Land," in *Dialogue* 49, no. 2 (Summer 2010): 115–122.

70. "Kairos," in *A Greek-English Lexicon of the New Testament and Other Early Christian Literature Second Edition,* eds. Walter Bauer, William F. Arndt, F. Wilbur Gingrich, and Frederick W. Danker (Chicago: University of Chicago Press, 1979), 394, 395.

71. Johnston, *The Manitous*, 6.

Chapter 2

Luther and Kenotic Space

WHY LUTHER?

Indigenous thinkers and theologians are wise, in my estimation, to query the utility of Western Christianity for a reclamation of place as a category for rethinking religious life in the 21st century. If Christianity has anything to offer, it will do so only in a chastened mode. It has done too much to misshape our present time, a time replete with a kind of forgetfulness of place that ushers in environment decay, a displaced spirituality and political chaos. The church, in concert with empire in many guises, has too often bulldozed over Indigenous worldviews, criminalized Indigenous religious traditions, and acted with a kind of paternalism that simply justifies Native suspicion of things Western, including the Christian tradition.

Vine Deloria Jr. and George "Tink" Tinker, discussed above, have been pioneering voices in challenging a Christian sense of self-importance and have brought North American Christians face to face with a difficult truth: others do not embrace what we hold dear. Tinker gives this a particularly sharp treatment in his discussions of Luther and Lutheranism, being especially critical of the law/gospel dialectic at the heart of Luther's theology.[1] As a Lutheran, this holds special interest for me. In what follows I provide an instance of how one might engage this critique in service of rethinking place for students of Luther. In what follows, readers will experience something of a dialectical engagement of Christian theology in its Lutheran expression and a critique of this. This will happen under the aegis of a respectful expectation that it is only by encountering the other that the self is resolved in both senses of the word: resolved as in "solved again" in self-discovery and resolved as in "resolved to do something" with a new impetus.

In sum, my foray in what follows is guided by an insight received from the recognition by Archbishop Mark MacDonald (the National Indigenous Archbishop of the Anglican Church of Canada) that global Christianity is being revitalized as it engages Indigenous religious traditions the world over in the humbled expectation that God is at work here, too.[2] In this chapter I begin with the presupposition that Christianity needs to reclaim fundamental truths anew by dialogue with Indigenous insights. These insights give fresh perspectives for rethinking place in theology. As I work through Indigenous criticisms of Christianity, and Lutheranism in particular, in this chapter, I will explore how such criticisms resurrect Luther's rich theology of creation. This theology of creation strikes an important counterpoint to the common reading of Luther as the proto-modern theologian, who paved the way for the buffered self, whose spirituality is so focused on the self-God relationship as to be blind to community and creation. I begin with a personal memory which raises questions about the famous (some say infamous) treatment of law/gospel in Lutheran thought. By revisiting this dialect in light of Indigenous insights, fresh perspectives on Luther's theology of creation are raised, which allow me to explore how kenosis as God's way of being shapes the contours of kairotic space.

HEARING HARD NEWS

As one might well expect, a Christian engaging Indigenous thought will hear a good bit of criticism of Christian belief and practice. At one level, Indigenous rejection of theological themes dear to my heart results in a kind of knee jerk reaction. At another level I understand, appreciate, and accept this in light of the horrid treatment of Native Americans by Christian settlers.[3] Yet something of the settler inside of me chafes. I want my religion to be wanted. Likewise, I also find myself, from time to time, being taken back to some of my experiences of Indigenous folk and their ways, and I recall with some pain my own rejection of some of their traditions, rites, etc.

I remember, in my first parish, St. Peter's Ecumenical, located in Northern Alberta in Slave Lake, a particular experience that sobers me. I was invited to be a part of a sentencing circle. This occurred in the early 1990s. Courts in the near North were backing up with first-time offenders who too regularly repeated their misdemeanors. It was proposed that a handful of communities be sites for a trial alternate sentencing system for first-time offenders who were youth. Judges had the latitude to redirect first-time offenders to groups of community members. We would sit in a circle, and listen first to those impacted by the crime, and then to the youth. Sentences were derived from the community and were intended to work at reconciling broken relationships between the offended and offender.

Slave Lake was chosen as a site, and I was invited to participate. There was some basic training in how the courts worked and what we could and couldn't do in alternate sentencing. It was an earlier time, and there was not much training in cultural sensitivity, which would certainly be included today. This would have been helpful since the North and Near North has a significant population of First Nation, Metis and Inuit residents. Fortunately, we had a couple of Indigenous folk in our circle, who taught us a bit about the culture of some of the youth we worked with. I learned a good bit in that circle about the importance of family, the role of reparation, and the path of reconciliation.

I remember one day coming to the meeting with a bad case of allergies. An elderly Cree woman, who was a part of the circle, told me she knew of some herbs that helped with allergies. I was interested in this and said so. She then told me that if I wanted to follow up with this, it would be appropriate for me to give her some tobacco, at which point she would share her knowledge with me. I thanked her, but never took her up on it. This was my first encounter with this practice, and I really didn't know what to make of it. Was it pagan? Would I betray my faith by doing this? Why wouldn't she just inform me about the remedy? If it was about recompense, surely money would be more appropriate, I thought. I had many questions but didn't know to whom they should be directed, afraid that they would be insulting to the elder and so I chose to respond to her gracious offer with silence. I have since come to understand a bit more about the role of tobacco, as a medicine from the Creator, and used as a sign of respect in asking another for assistance, or a teaching. But at that point, I found it a bit off-putting, a response I have had from time to time as I have encountered Indigenous ways that I have not understood. Some of the protocols have seemed to me to be legalistic, and I must admit that, at times, I have been judgmental about beliefs and practices that were unfamiliar. In part, I instantiated the very thing that worries Tinker. In the citation noted above, he draws particular attention to the Lutheran use of the law/gospel dialectic, which I think—in retrospect—informed my unease.

ANOTHER KIND OF LAW

The law/gospel dialectic, simply put, works on the premise that there are two principal ways in which God gives us the law.[4] The first use of the law is termed the civil use and speaks to the gift of government, God's ordering of the cosmos, as well as the civil and natural laws which order and make possible the flourishing of humanity and creation. The second use of the law names God's expectations of us: how we ought to live in light of God's promises. Luther and his compatriots understood that the second use of the law served to underscore human inability to be what we are created to be. Human response to the law is in the mode of despair—at our (correct) realization that we cannot fulfill the law—or pride in our (mistaken) assumption that we are doing very well with the law. When the law has done its proper work, the contrite sinner is ready to hear the gospel, announcing God's unconditional love given in Christ to faith. Tinker notes,

> Yet this intrinsic emphasis on human sin and sinfulness violates Indian people in two devastating ways. First of all, Indian cultures do not inherently share the same sense of human depravity that is so pervasive in European cultures and has there given rise to the doctrine of original sin. . . . Second, and more important, given the social dysfunctionality that reigns in Indian communities as a result of our history of colonialism and oppression, this emphasis on sin and depravity impedes any hearing of the good news among a people demoralized both spiritually and emotionally by their experience of conquest.[5]

Tinker's rejection of this way in which the Lutheran dialectic of law and gospel is used is important, and in many ways taken up by Luther himself, who would counsel pastors to console hearts broken by personal and social dysfunction rather than condemn those already condemned.[6] Yet it is common for Protestants—certainly Lutheran Protestants—to fixate on how we fail in our spiritual life. Consequently, we sometimes fail both to hear the gospel and how the word "law" is differently used in other contexts, and how it also references God's intention for the well-being of the cosmos. We too often understand as "legalistic" the uses of laws that are decidedly not. A case in point is "The Great Law of Peace" from my own context.

Rick Monture, a Haudenosaunee scholar from The Six Nations of the Grand River Nation, writes of the establishment of this foundational law by the Peacemaker.[7] The story is told that after creation, humans began to disregard their responsibility of giving thanks to the Creator for the gift of life, and so a number of rites were given them to reinforce their relationships with all of creation. After a long period of time, the people fell into conflict and in the historic territory of the Haudenosaunee peoples in what is now New York State, five nations developed who warred despite a clan system tying them to one another. On the other side of Lake Ontario, a Huron woman gave birth to a son who spent much time by himself. At one point his mother and grandmother followed him and found him making a canoe from stone. When they asked him what he was going to do with it, he replied that people on the other side of the lake were in need of him, and so he would cross the lake in this canoe in service of them. He did precisely this despite the misgiving of his family and did so in service of bringing peace to the Five Nations. For this reason, he was called "The Peacemaker."

At the heart of the Peacemaker's teaching is "the social, spiritual, and political structures of peace, power, and righteousness."[8] The Peacemaker endured a number of tests by which he demonstrated his legitimate authority, as he brought first four, then five nations into a confederacy (later a sixth joined).[9] He instructed these nations to name themselves "Haudenosaunee," which means "we build the house (together)" since part of his instructions included the establishment of longhouses in which they lived and which served as a cipher for the Great Law under which they lived.[10] Another important symbol for these was the Great Tree of Peace, under which all nations could "seek refuge and an alternative to violence and war."[11] Monture summarizes the importance of the Great Law of Peace when he writes:

> To the Haudenosaunee, the story of the Peacemaker and his message is evidence of the power that is created when human beings set their minds to achieve something beneficial and good for all. It was this message of goodness that the Peacemaker shared with the Five Nations long ago and it is the guiding principle that continues to influence decision making among the Confederacy Chiefs and Clanmothers to this day.[12]

At the core of this description of the Great Law of Peace is an understanding of "law" as a way of living together that is an alternate to "violence and war." Law is here not first a moral overseer, or a pedagogue. It is primarily political, and it creates space for the flourishing of human community. At first blush, that might seem far removed from the use of "law" in Lutheran circles. Yet such an estimation is unnecessarily restrictive in light of Luther's appeal to the first use of the law. Gustaf Wingren, to cite one scholar of Luther, notes how the law is "love in motion," and so need not be understood in a condemnatory tone alone.[13] Wingren wrote in the context of a mid-20th-century movement that has since been identified as "Scandinavian Creation Theology."[14] We turn now to consider insights from this movement, and how they might engage the Haudenosaunee use of "law" in the Great Law of Peace.

After the First World War, Karl Barth's theology, with its attenuated critique of culture by way of Christology, was discerned by many to be a faithful response to a too-common collusion of Christianity with the machinations of empire. Barth's focus on revelation and Christology as doctrinal touchstones was applauded by many as a necessary corrective to the sorts of theological and ecclesial deficiencies that produced the so-called "German Christians" who capitulated to the Führer's demands and vision for Germany.[15] Barth's pen can be discerned in the *Barmen Declaration*'s "Nein!" to the demands of the church by proponents of National Socialism. Barth rejected any "point of contact" between theology and culture, whereby one might be bent to the will of the other. Students of theology will know well of the debate between Barth and Brunner on this front, and will also be aware of the important distinctions between his theology and that of Paul Tillich, especially as it was received in North America. But in Northern Europe an important response to Barth was developed in the work of theologians Gustaf Wingren, and Regin Prenter, and the philosopher Knud Løgstrup, who paid special attention to Luther's theology of creation.

CREATION AND KENOSIS

In an early work titled *Law and Gospel*, Wingren critiques Barth's inversion of the law/gospel dialectic.[16] Barth, following what he took to be Reformation sensibilities about grace, presumed that the law (what God asks of us) can only be heard after we have received the liberating word of the gospel (what God promises us in Christ). The gospel, then, according to Barth, has priority both logically and temporarily in Christian thought and discourse. Wingren countered, in the mid-part of the 20th century, that this inversion has unintended consequences that outstrip the effect of assuaging unnecessary guilt. Wingren associated the word "law" with both uses as per Luther. By under-narrating "law," neo-Orthodox theologians under-stress the importance of creation since creation is itself an instance of God's natural law. And so the first use of law also includes the very architecture of creation. The word "architecture" is used quite deliberately here insofar as an architect is a master of place. Their vocation is to organize space to facilitate human flourishing, with the house being a primordial instance. For this reason Gaston Bachelard can write that "the house is one of the greatest powers of integration for the thoughts, memories and dreams of mankind."[17] The *oikos* of humankind, however, is the *cosmos*, which has its own poetics of integration. Creation, then, is heard to speak as the Creator makes place for humankind alongside the rest of the created order. Our place within this order is circumscribed by the law (in the sense of the first use of the law), given us as a gift.

This "law" needs to be affirmed even before we hear of the "gospel." To return to the convictions of the Scandinavian Creation Theologians of the mid-20th century, Barth's focus on Christology also ran against the logic of the Creed and did not give the beginning of the biblical narrative the attention it demanded.[18] Further, Wingren considered that Barth's way of looking at texts and doctrine had additional problems. Chief among these was that salvation was primarily construed as knowledge rather than healing.[19] Wingren considered Luther's interest in Christology not to be primarily about revelation, but considered Luther to follow Irenaeus, with his focused attention on recapitulation and the mending of the universe.[20] Moreover, following Luther,

Wingren understood this creation to be one that is continuous.[21] Creation was not a discrete act at the beginning of time but is an ongoing reality at the foundation of our experience. Creation was the very act of God making space for all of the created order and re-creation was understood to be a restoration after the destructive dis-placement of sin. The Scandinavian Creation Theologians were very fond of Irenaeus's attention to a soteriology of recapitulation, insofar as it pictured Christ re-placing creation under his divine headship.[22]

In sum, Wingren invited his readers to take creation seriously and to consider human sin in terms of environmental consequences rather than narrowly reading sin in moralistic categories. This reduction of sin to morality is a perspective roundly rejected by many Indigenous thinkers, insofar as Indigenous spiritualities recognize that brokenness is about relationship rather than rules, and since among our most important relationship is with the land, the environment is an especially important consideration. This perspective serves to correct many Christians, who construe sin as a moral category and make of the body a problem to be ordered by the soul. The Bible, alas, is somewhat ambiguous on this front.

On the one hand, God's embrace of the human condition in the flesh of Jesus has been understood as a profound affirmation of the worldly nature of being human.[23] Christology is not the only place wherein this affirmation is reflected. Another important theological locus would be the manner in which the Christian church generally has understood the significance of sacraments, wherein matter is deemed to be capable of bearing the divine word of grace to humans. So, on the one hand, we have a significant and profound affirmation of the corporeality of human existence in that bread, water, and wine used alongside word to communicate the gospel. In this instance, matter matters.

The other side of the coin, however, is not necessarily so positive. In this instance, Christians are regularly reminded of the danger of the flesh. In more extreme instances of this prejudice against the flesh, the flesh is seen as the weak point wherein sin makes its entry into the human community. Not a few of the church fathers pointed to sexuality as the primordial instance of human sin and weakness, and the doctrine of original sin as understood by certain fathers presumed that the state of sinfulness was transmitted by the act of sexual intercourse. Sex itself was and is deemed sinful.[24] Despite recent exegetical efforts to underscore that the word "flesh" is used by Paul as a cipher for a way of existing wherein the self rather than God is at the center, a broader distrust of the flesh creeps continually into the Christian tradition. We see this, for instance, in the following quotation from Luther himself, in which he exegetes Psalm 8.

> This is what it really means to live in heaven, not with the body but with the heart and the soul in faith and hope. By faith in the Word, our heart has taken

hold of life in heaven through the power of the Holy Spirit. But we must still wait till the Last Day, when our old "bag of worms" will finally be purified and come along, too. Now the flesh still clings to us, and our soul is still languishing in a dark prison, so that it cannot see the glory of our homeland and inheritance in heaven. When the prison is shattered, then we shall see it, not in part through a mirror darkly, but perfectly and face to face, as St. Paul says, 1 Corinthians 13:12.[25]

Passages such as this problematize the body. The body is a burden, needing to be purified. And yet, it is worth noting two themes in Luther here that allow us to reframe our reading of the body in Luther in particular and in the Christian tradition in general. First, it is to be noted that Luther anticipates a resurrection of the flesh that affirms the body's value even though it needs to be purified. Unlike platonic thought, which deemed the body to be beyond redemption, and finally that from which the soul was to be freed, the body in Christian thought is to be resurrected, and as such purified. But a still more important point is that Luther's understanding of the human being was one in which sin is not a contagion of the body, reined in by the soul, but rather that the whole human, body and soul, is under the strain and stain of sin, to be made whole in Christ who heals the whole human.

> In the interpretation of *Magnificat*, [Luther's] starting point is 1 Thess 5:23, where the Apostle Paul presents the anthropological trichotomy of the spirit, the soul, and the body. According to Paul, the whole human being, including these three "parts" may become holy. Luther points out that the whole human being as well as all these three parts, is also differentiated into two aspects called spirit and flesh. The first division refers to human nature, and the second to its qualities. Accordingly, human nature has three parts, all of which may be holy or unholy, good or evil. To be spirit in the qualitative sense means to be good, and to be flesh in this sense refers to wickedness.[26]

The whole human is, according to Luther, under the dominion of sin, subject to the taunts of death and the devil. Yet herein we find a significant point of difference from Indigenous thinkers who are more inclined to believe in an original wholeness. Rupert Ross, in giving an account of the Ojibway understanding of being human, notes the following in discussing the differences between Western approaches to justice with those of First Peoples:

> If it is your conviction that people live one short step from hell, that it is more natural to sin than to do good, then your response as a judicial official will be to use terror to prevent the taking of the last step backward. . . . If, by contrast, it is your conviction that people live one step away from heaven, you will be

more likely to respond by coaxing them gently forward, by encouraging them to progress, to realize the goodness within them. The use of coercion, threats or punishment by those who would serve as guides to goodness would seem a denial of the very vision that inspires them.[27]

Ross has articulated what is elsewhere used to underscore a fundamental difference between traditional Native and Christian worldviews. It is not my intent to prove the superiority of one or the other of these positions; nor is it my intent to flatten the difference between the two; rather, what I hope to do in what follows is to allow the difference to bring into relief Luther's treatment of the human so that the reality of sin is not seen to be a rejection of created reality. In so doing, I turn now to another Nordic interpreter of Luther: Regin Prenter.

Many years ago Regin Prenter wrote a profoundly important work on Luther called *Spiritus Creator*.[28] In it, he exegeted some of Luther's most important works on the role of the Holy Spirit in Luther's theology. As the title indicates, the Holy Spirit is seen to be the force of creation. Further, the work indicates the manner in which the Spirit ever works in concert with the Word at the bidding of the Father. Eeva Markikainen has noted that this insight leads to understanding "kenosis" as a Trinitarian activity for Luther:

> God gives himself in three ways: in creation, in Christ, and in the working of the Spirit both inwardly and outwardly. . . . The train of all of Luther's baptismal theology is clearly expressed in his understanding of the gift of baptism as the total gift of God's presence and salvation.[29]

This is, of course, an astounding image of the Holy Trinity. The Western theological tradition has typically reserved the theme of kenosis for the second person of the Trinity, to the end that redemption has been understood as the event wherein God's self-giving is revealed as an act of retrieval. The incarnation alone, then, is seen to be kenotic. Yet it might be argued that insofar as the Holy Trinity is understood to be a Trinity in unity and unity in Trinity, the patristic adage *opera deus unum sint* holds for *all* of God's activity: creation as well as redemption. And so, there is a certain "kenosis" already in creation, wherein God is encountered in each place—already at work in advance of our knowing it to be so.

This image of the work of the Triune God allows us to see the world differently. We have a place to be because God has made space for us in the divine self. Space itself is a trace of the divine, such that we now know that our taking place is by virtue of divine kenosis. God empties the divine self so that we might have a place to be. All place bears the character of kenosis. In commenting on the first article of the Apostles' Creed, Luther notes:

> For here we see how the Father has given to us himself with all creation and has abundantly provided for us in this life, apart from the fact that he has also showered us with inexpressible eternal blessings through is Son and the Holy Spirit, as we shall hear.[30]

For Luther, the kenotic language of Philippians 2: 5–8 follows a pattern already existent in creation. God made space within God and so space, place, and land are already holy. Moreover, this pattern has profound significance for a theological anthropology. Luther notes in *The Freedom of the Christian*:

> Although the Christian is thus free from all works, he ought in this liberty to empty himself, take upon himself the form of a servant, be made in the likeness of men, be found in human form, and to serve, help, and in every way deal with his neighbor as he sees that God through Christ has dealt and still deals with him. This he should do freely, having regard for nothing but divine approval.[31]

This quotation points to Luther's vision of a kenotic public space wherein humans mirror God by serving their neighbors. Just as God makes space for us, we are called to make space for others. The God who gives the divine self in creation also gives the divine self in Christ and this pathway of self-giving is given us by the Holy Spirit. We are shaped by a care for others that is informed by the phenomenon of trust, which is at the heart of being human. This theme has been explored by the Danish philosopher Knut Løgstrup whose phenomenology of ethics elucidates what public space reveals about God's creative activity: God creates humans in a condition of trust that mitigates a thoroughly pessimistic view of human community and, so, public space.

Løgstrup provides us with some useful resources for thinking through what it means to be in the human community. He is a philosopher who provides a phenomenology of human community that works out of the presupposition that human life regularly demonstrates a fundamental sense of trust in our dealings with one another. His astounding book *The Ethical Demand* begins with the observation:

> It is characteristic of human life that we normally encounter one another with natural trust. This is true not only in the case of persons who are well acquainted with one another but also in the case of complete strangers. Only because of some special circumstances do we ever distrust a stranger in advance. . . . We never suspect a person of falsehood until after we have caught him in a lie.[32]

In a fashion, as Løgstrup ponders what it means to be human, he recognizes that the primordial nature of human community is fundamentally grounded in trust. Trust is, in a way, a kenotic activity built into the very architecture of creation. The hallowed nature of space reminds us that God has entrusted a place to us. God's primordial posture toward us is trust, and so we are able to mirror that in our day to day encounters. Trust is the primary condition that makes it possible to negotiate public space. If I did not trust my fellow drivers, I would never get in a car. We cannot conceive a public space that endures aside from a significant trust that grounds relationships. Trust is ever and always a giving of the self to the other. The concept of the public and public space points to God's promise to the cosmos, a promise which elicits our trust. And so both the trust that makes human community possible and the faith that makes communion with God possible are grounded in God's gift of the Spirit, who both creates and recreates kenotic space of care.

THE POETIC SPIRIT

My turn to the Spirit at this point in this chapter may strike some as odd, given Luther's battles with those whom he disparagingly called the *Schwärmer*, who self-identified as Anabaptist: those reformers who felt that the Holy Spirit was leading them in new directions. Luther would often quip that they had swallowed the Holy Spirit, feathers and all, in his rebuttal of what he deemed their spiritual enthusiasm. Luther was not, however, uninterested in the Holy Spirit. He asserted that for those who live by grace through faith, the Spirit can serve Christian theology in ways both ancient and new. Consider the following quotation from Luther in his introduction to Psalm 111, where he recalls his decision to set aside his desire to write a hymn for the purpose of Christian instruction:

> But the Holy Spirit, the greatest and best Poet, had already composed better and finer hymns, namely, the precious psalms, to thank and praise God. Therefore I gave up my own wretched and worthless poetry and took up this psalm, the Holy Spirit's hymn and poem, expounding it as His own instruction to us on the manner and language in which we ought to thank and praise God for His grace, especially for the holy Sacrament.[33]

Luther's identification of the Spirit as Poet has more significance than might appear at first glance. At one level, readers might be inclined to imagine that the Spirit as Poet is simply Luther's way of saying that the Spirit wrote scriptures, and so by extension, the Psalms, and this Psalm in particular. Yet this is not enough, and in fact, leaving this text in this fashion will only lead down difficult roads insofar as it allows, if not encourages, exegetes of Luther to read into his text a doctrine of plenary inspiration that expunges from Luther's view of scripture the notion that it is rather like a crib cradling the infant Christ. Luther has a nuanced view of scripture. And so, in exegeting this passage, we need to keep in mind that Luther's references to poets in his writing more generally reference the great pagan poets of antiquity. The word "poetry" has this reference on the one hand, while on the other it always carries within it its etymological referent in the Greek word for "to make." These two notions together invite us to ponder the probability that when we hear Luther speak of the Holy Spirit as Poet, especially in light of the theme of *Spiritus Creator*, we need to imagine that the Spirit as author of the poetry of the psalms is but one instance—certainly an important instance—of the Spirit's broader poetic, or creative, work: the Spirit creating the world is divine poetry as well. The psalms read in this fashion would, then, be seen to be a concentration of the experience of life, which seems to be the very thing that poetry does. It is, indeed, this understanding of poetry—rather than poetry as ornamentation—that points out that poetry, in some fashion, catches the essence of life or the architecture of creation.[34] Life, like poetry, is a mystery—it is experienced in its sounding, in its *announcing* itself.[35] Life *is* in its happening, however fleeting that may be. And while this image underscores how ephemeral our life is, poetry, in its witness to this evasiveness, points to what "living" *is*: living is stepping out in trust and so wagering the self—living kenotically. Trust names the mystery of human life that we experience *in situ*, in certain places with concrete experiences. The poetic Spirit creates space for us to wager a word, to enter into the phenomenon of communicating: now with a sound, now with a gesture, now with a touch.

Communication is the primordial mode of existence of both church and world. Communication is correlative to the kenotic phenomenon of caring trust in that our speaking is always a giving up and giving over of the self in one mode or another. But a difference obtains between church and the world in that the church that speaks/confesses that it is spoken by the poetic Spirit. And yet, when the church speaks authentically it speaks in harmony with creation and so knows both the stories of its constitution in the Bible and the tale of its arrival on the land in which it finds itself: it lives out of its stories and it lives its stories *in situ*.

Just as Indigenous stories always "take place" seriously by referencing loci, so a telling of the gospel takes place in reference to its context and to the space carved by pulpit, altar, and font. Both places—the place of worship and the space holding that worship place—merge with poetic potency. Yet, we might ask, how does all of this bear upon a reclamation of place?

Løgstrup provides us with an analysis of poetry in which he suggests that poetry relates form and content in a fashion that discloses rather than informs.[36] He also notes, however, that disclosure is always by way of *indirect* expression. In this, poetry is third to language as semantic and directly expressive.³⁷ He also notes that philosophy clarifies experiences while poetry makes them present.³⁸ But presence always presumes place. Poetry sketches places for us. But it does so in a manner that is both disclosive and indirect. Poetry makes the familiar unfamiliar again by drawing our attention to what is so close to us that it has become invisible. We see where we are with new eyes and so with a new vision of its promise, the very condition of the possibility for our trust.

Poetic space, then, is roomy. Yet we know that room is only made by removing. There is always a burial, a hiding, a forgetting that occurs in poetic space. Space that allows for illumination cannot be cluttered. Place becomes spacious by way of sacrifice. Certain things are left behind, or ignored, or perhaps even obliterated in order that spaciousness arrives. There is, however, a certain danger in this. Who decides what is eliminated? Who decides what is disclosed? This invites us to ponder the question of ethics, insofar as place is only poetically spacious insofar as it is ethically construed. The poet Lorna Crozier writes that "resistance is often the place where poetry starts."³⁹ Resistance, of course, always refers to a relationship—a being together by our being over-against. The Spirit works the world by writing verse as both re*vers*al and con*vers*ation. The Spirit works us by placing us in the world kenotically, where caring trust is our primordial posture that aims at a living in harmony with one another and the cosmos. This is not to gainsay the denial of this trust in the brokenness of creation, but still a wistfulness accompanies its betrayal and so shadows of trust and the kenotic space that undergird it remain.⁴⁰ Even in our brokenness a shattered vision of the world as one endures: the places we live in continue to call us to give ourselves in care, and poetically after the fashion of the poetic Spirit, who speaks of the God who gives the divine self to the end that we discover that every place is ripe with kenotic possibility. Place is finally kairotic because it has been shaped by the kenotic God who calls us to give ourselves *in situ* for God's glory and for creation's good.

CONCLUSION

Luther's theology, when read in concert with Indigenous insights, invites his students to attend to certain key themes with special interest in questions of place. We explored how he takes seriously the created world to be an instantiation of the kenotic activity of God. We also explored how natural and civil laws instantiate God's will for ethical space to be formed in human community attentive to the well-being of all the world and how trust names our primordial experience of place. Lastly, we read with Luther of the poetic Spirit, who is ever ordering the world to make of place a space wherein a kind of harmony obtains in life lived together justly. In what follows we will explore what harmonious space might look like using insights from Friedrich Schleiermacher, a thinker indebted—in certain ways—to Luther and yet drastically different in orientation.

NOTES

1. Tinker, *American Indian Liberation*, 90.
2. Bishop Mark MacDonald, "Day of Dialogue" (lecture, Waterloo Lutheran Seminary, November 3, 2011).
3. I use the term "settler" to reference people who are not Indigenous to this land but distinguish it from the "settled," which references African-Americans and African-Canadians who were brought to Turtle Island against their will. I speak of immigrants, refugees, etc., as "those settling." I am mindful that these broad categorizations are not exact. Moreover, I use the term "settler" in a non-pejorative sense, even while the fact of the matter is that all who settle have displaced those Indigenous to the land. I am grateful to Mirko Petricevic for conversations regarding this distinction.
4. "Gospel" names God's unconditional acceptance of us despite our failure to follow the "law," which names what God expects of us—in the two modes discussed here. Some Lutherans, in concert with the Reformed tradition, argue for a third use of the law, the discussion of which is beyond the scope of the present work.
5. Tinker, *American Indian Liberation*, 90.
6. Marit Trelstad, informed by a feminist perspective, argues that the misuse of the law-gospel demands that we revisit its use and commends a gospel-law-gospel hermeneutic. She notes that the law-gospel dialectic "presents a model of coercive power that lacks genuine authority and therefore efficacy." See Marit Trelstad, "Charity Terror Begins at Home: Luther and the 'Terrifying and Killing' Law," in *Lutherrenaisance Past and Present,* eds. Christine Helmer and Bo Kristian Holm (Göttingen: Vandenhoeck & Ruprecht, 2015), 209. She also distinguishes Luther's descriptive functions from performative ones of the law, concluding that the former is amenable to "feminist concerns for truth-telling and accountability" while the latter should be rejected since it "offers a dynamic of abuse as a model of God" (Ibid., 210). Other examples of rereading Luther and the Lutheran tradition can be found in Else Marie Wiberg Pedersen (ed.), *The Alternative Luther: Lutheran Theology from the Subaltern* (Lanham, MD: Lexington/Fortress, 2019); Mary J. Streufert (ed.), *Transformative Lutheran Theologies: Feminist, Womanist, and Mujerista Perspectives* (Minneapolis, MN: Fortress Press, 2010); Deanna Thompson, *Crossing the Divide: Luther, Feminism, and the Cross* (Minneapolis, MN: Fortress Press, 2004); and Paul S. Chung, Ulrich Duchrow, and Craig Nessan, *Liberating Lutheran Theology: Freedom for Justice and Solidarity with Others in a Global Context* (Minneapolis, MN: Fortress Press, 2011).

7. Rick Monture, *We Share our Matters: Two Centuries of Writing and Resistance at Six Nations of the Grand River* (Winnipeg: University of Manitoba Press, 2014). In what follows I draw upon this work. See especially pp. 6–11. Alternate accounts of the Peacemaker exist. One, in which he is identified as Mohawk, can be found in William N. Fenton, *The Great Law and the Longhouse: A Political History of the Iroquois Confederacy* (Norman: University of Oklahoma Press, 1998), 59–64.

8. Ibid., 7. See also Alfred, *Peace, Power, Righteousness*.

9. The first four were the Mohawk, Oneida, Cayuga, and Seneca nations. Shortly thereafter the Onandaga joined. Later still, the Tuscarora joined to make it the Six Nations.

10. Monture, *We Share Our Matters*, 9.

11. Ibid., 10.

12. Ibid.

13. Gusaf Wingren, *Credo: The Christian View of Faith and Life*. trans. Edgar M. Carlson (Minneapolis, MN: Augsburg, 1981), 63.

14. See Niels Henrik Gregersen, Bengt Kristensson Uggla, and Trygve Wyller (eds.), *Reformation Theology for a Post-Secular Age: Løgstrup, Prenter, Wingren, and the Future of Scandinavian Creation Theology* (Göttingen: Vandenhoek & Ruprecht, 2017).

15. For an important analysis of the misuse of Luther in this, see Christine Helmer, *How Luther Became the Reformer* (Louisville, KY: Westminster/John Knox, 2019) and James M. Stayer, *Martin Luther: German Saviour: German Evangelical Theological Factions and the Interpretation of Luther, 1917–1933* (Montreal and Kingston: McGill-Queens University Press, 2000).

16. Gustaf Wingren, *Creation and Law*, trans. Ross MacKenzie (Philadelphia: Muhlenberg Press, 1961), 11, 41, 186.

17. Bachelard, *The Poetics of Space*, trans. Maria Jolas (Boston: Beacon Press, 1994), 6.

18. Wingren, *Creation and Law*, 41.

19. Gustaf Wingren, *Creation and Gospel: The New Situation European Theology* (Toronto: Edwin Mellen Press, 1979), 39.

20. Ibid., 48, 43, 28.

21. Ibid., 26–28.

22. Christine Svinth-Værge Pöder, "Regin Prenter and Scandinavian Creation Theology," in *Reformation Theology for a Post-Secular Age*, 79 notes how Prenter, for example, "rejects the common divisions between sacred and secular, between salvation history and world history."

23. Further to this, see Elisabeth Gerle, *Passionate Embrace: Luther on Love, Body and Sensual Presence* (Eugene, OR: Cascade, 2017).

24. See Pamela Dickey Young, "Moving Critical Theologies from Descriptive Discourses into Constructive Spaces," in *Intersecting Voices*, 361.

25. Martin Luther, *Luther's Works, American Edition, 55 Volumes*, eds. Jaroslav Pelikan (vols. 1–30) and Helmut Lehmann (vols. 31–55) (Philadelphia, PA: Fortress and St. Louis: Concordia, 1955–86). Hereafter indicated by LW. See LW 12, 105, 6.

26. Antii Raunio, in *Engaging Luther: A (New) Theological Assessment*, ed. Olli-Pekka Vainio (Eugene, OR: Cascade Books, 2010), pp. 42–43.

27. Ross, *Dancing with a Ghost*, 194.

28. Regin Prenter, *Spiritus Creator,* trans. John M. Jensen (Philadelphia: Muhlenberg Press, 1951.

29. See Eeva Martikainen, "Baptism," in *Engaging Luther*, 96. See also Christine Helmer, *The Trinity and Martin Luther: Revised Edition* (Bellingham, WA: Lexham Press, 2017).

30. Robert Kolb and Timothy J. Wengert, *Book of Concord: The Confessions of the Evangelical Lutheran Church* (Minneapolis, MN: Fortress Press, 2000), 433.

31. LW 31, 366.

32. Knut Løgstrup, *The Ethical Demand*, Introduction by Hans Fink and Alasdair MacIntyre, various trans. (Notre Dame, IN: University of Notre Dame Press, 1997) 8.

33. LW 13, 351. Luther's rejection of his own poetic capacity here is, finally, a rhetorical device. In addition to his theological works he composed lyrics for hymns and demonstrated a mastery of the German language that advanced the development of a standard *Hochdeutsch*.

34. And so Bachelard notes that poetry offers us "primal images," which "give us back areas of being, houses in which the human being's certainty of being is concentrated, and we have the impression that, by living in such images as these, in images that are as stabilizing as these are, we could start a new life, a life that would be our very own, what would belong to us in our very depths." *The Poetics of Space*, 33.

35. See LW 13, 119: "Furthermore, this simile is most appropriate in either of two ways, whether one understands it as referring to essence or motion. With respect to its essence, no one knows what speech is. It is a sound which touches the ear. Yet neither its beginning nor its end is known. Nor is it known what it is or where it originates. Before one begins to speak, the sound is nothingness. When one ceases to speak, it is nothingness. Apart from its sound, we know nothing about the nature of speech."

36. Løgstrup, *Ethical Demand*, 192,193,197.

37. Ibid., 198, 199.

38. Ibid., 205.

39. Lorna Crozier, "Afterword," in *The Poetry of Lorna Crozier*, ed. Catherine Hunter (Waterloo: WLU Press, 2005), 56.

40. See Allen G. Jorgenson, "Martin Luther in Scandinavian Creation Theology," in *Reformation Theology for a Post-Secular Age*.

Chapter 3

Schleiermacher and Harmonic Place

PIONEER OF MODERN PROTESTANT THEOLOGY

If the wisdom of engaging Luther in conversation with Indigenous insights seemed curious, the deployment of Schleiermacher for the same purpose may be seen as odd to the extreme. Modern Protestant theology, especially in the guise of the liberal tradition that many trace back to Schleiermacher, has a problematic relationship with First Nations in North America. The difficulties can be seen as both direct and indirect.

Directly, practitioners of traditional religions could point to Schleiermacher's tendency to go with the currents of his time, which used an evolutionary model of the religions to make sense of their plurality. Like Hegel, Schleiermacher imagined that religious life evolved from fetishism through to polytheism, to variants on monotheism and finally achieving the apex of religious sensibility in the Christian religion.[1]

The indirect critique is perhaps more insidious and, for that reason, especially significant: as the so-called Father of Protestant Christianity, Schleiermacher is more generally identified with the great liberal Protestant tradition which took for granted the ascendency of the Western cultures and mores. This intellectual force helped to fuel expansionism in the 19th and 20th centuries, with his pioneering work in theology, hermeneutics, philosophy, and more, along with his popular and widely read translation of Plato. Moreover, Schleiermacher is more generally identified with that kind of Protestantism which is fixated on religious affections—religion in the guise of feeling—that has been identified with the worst of relativism giving rise to reactionary fundamentalisms that have been toxic for Indigenous religions. This description is more broadly of a piece with a critique that collapses Schleiermacher's thought into occidental exceptionalism. Why would Indigenous peoples even want to read Schleiermacher, never mind engage him creatively, and why would I dare to bring these two streams of thought together? Why indeed, and yet an entrée is suggested in a reader on Indigenous theology:

> Schleiermacher's approach to biblical understanding, featuring a reconstruction of the author's mental process, provides a way of introducing Indian cultural values into an understanding of Christian practices.[2]

Some Indigenous theologians, then, see some utility in the work of Schleiermacher, despite his identification with 19th-century liberalism. His attention to experience, his intentional hermeneutical approach to theology, and his interest in creative retrieval of tradition all commend themselves here. But before considering his contributions, it is important to address some of the dangers noted above.

The predominant reading of Schleiermacher that has pervaded North American and European schools more generally flows from a caricature of him as advanced by Barth, and more recently, by certain post-liberal thinkers. Barth's turn to revelation in response to the failure of liberal Protestant Christianity in the face of German expansionism in the early 20th century is an important marker in the history of contemporary theology. Yet, it is simplistic, and indeed, inaccurate simply to lay the failure of the co-option of the Protestant Church in Germany at the feet of Schleiermacher.

The historical development of Protestant theology in the 19th century involved twists and turns that sometimes carried Schleiermacher's thought in directions wholly disconnected with his own project. Moreover, the common critique of post-liberal thought, wherein Schleiermacher's theology is simply equated with a kind of experiential-expressive theology that is utterly subjective in nature, is far too simplistic.[3] Indeed, the tendency to bifurcate theological traditions into those wherein historically faithful religious paradigms presume that religious language shapes religious experience, and modern and relativistic paradigms, wherein religious experience shapes religious language is too simple, not to mention unfaithful to Schleiermacher, who is typically identified with the latter position.[4] I hold to a position wherein religious language and experience advance in some sort of a dialectical relationship,[5] a point I learned from Schleiermacher, who advanced the proposal that "Christianity is a language-forming principle."[6] This, in sum, brings us to an important reason to take Schleiermacher seriously in thinking through place alongside Indigenous sensibilities: He takes the category of experience seriously as a theological datum.[7] Schleiermacher, then, really does offer an alternative to the doctrinal propositionalism that Lindbeck properly critiques, yet his is not simply a mushy experiential expressivism, but a dialectically ordered exposition of experience in light of the Church's identification of Jesus as the Christ. This is something that can be quite helpful. Yet, what of the first critique: that of his conception of religions evolving with Christianity at the apex?

In responding to this important critique of Schleiermacher I offer three points. First, it simply must be admitted that in this instance Schleiermacher echoed his *Zeitgeist*, all the while recalling that in the context of the 19th century this approach was an advance over the more common vision of viewing other religious groups as simply misguided attempts to reach God at best, and at worst, demonic. All the same, readers of Schleiermacher need to pay attention to his slip into this way of viewing religion. Second, it is to be noted that Schleiermacher was open to positive possibilities evident in other religions and eschewed religious uniformity.[8] The religions more generally reflect what Schleiermacher understands to be the architecture of the universe: the dialectical relationship between the one and the many, wherein the common modern occidental propensity to favor the one over the many is deferred in favor of a dynamic tension.[9] Third, Schleiermacher's view of soteriology was such that religious sensibilities did not bear upon the question of eternal salvation. In his treatment of the doctrine of predestination, we find him advancing in a creative manner a kind of universalism that makes sense of the one and the many. The consequence of this is that if one reads the religions alongside reading Schleiermacher, one is given the luxury of exploring the utility of the religions toward an end other than salvation, since the Redeemer has addressed this.[10]

As an additional proviso to the above, let me be clear that I am not using Schleiermacher in a prescriptive fashion, imagining that he is exactly what the Indigenous community needs. Nothing is further from the truth. I leave it to this community to determine what is needed in their context. Contemporary non-Indigenous theologians, however, who work within the broad Western Protestant tradition have to deal with the tradition that has been inherited. It cannot simply be jettisoned without further ado. The 19th century is in the DNA of the mainline denominations in North America and Northern Europe. A fulsome reckoning with the strengths and weaknesses of this part of our history requires revisiting significant. In what follows, this is done in an ad hoc fashion on the theological topic under discussion. A theological project that is going to press toward its margins in service of truth needs to be mindful of the resources at its disposal, all the while attending to the perils and possibilities of this.

In what follows, I will explore Schleiermacher's thought with an eye on insights from Indigenous thinkers, all the while teasing out what I deem to be useful themes from Schleiermacher for making sense of place. By way of anticipation let me simply point to what will be explored in the following:

the way in which place relates to space, the importance of harmony, and the role of intuition/feeling in the thought of Schleiermacher. The first invites us to consider further what was discussed in the first chapter. The second point attains to what Randy Woodley has identified as the Harmony Way of Indigenous traditions.[11] The final point allows us to imagine that our way into truth, while including the cognitive dimension of human experience, is not restricted to the intellect, a point affirmed in Indigenous traditions the world over and the condition for the possibility of the embrace of the finite, and so space, place, and land.

PLACE AND TRUTH

As noted above, Schleiermacher worked with Plato's thought throughout his career, and so this philosophical source was influential on his thought.[12] His was not an uncritical acceptance of the platonic world, but from Plato and his confreres he shares the idea that the categories of truth, goodness, and beauty are inescapable themes to ponder for those who consider the human condition. Schleiermacher as theologian, philosopher, aesthete, and preacher dealt with them as surely as his forebears and contemporaries. Schleiermacher's thoughts on truth, good, and beauty are accessible to the English reader in *Dialectic*, *Lectures on Philosophy of Ethics*, and *Speeches to Cultured Despisers* (in concert with *Soliloquies*).[13] In what follows I will comment on this triad, attentive to the theme of place as it emerges in these treatments.

Schleiermacher's *Dialectic, or the Art of Doing Philosophy* sketches out dialectic as the path to knowing what is true.[14] It does this by paying attention to the human experience of thinking, claiming that—in contrast to Kant—the rules by which we think, and the conditions for the possibility of thought "do not admit of distinction."[15] In other words, how it is that we think (the condition for thought, or what Schleiermacher calls the transcendental component of thought) and how we think (the act of thought, or what he calls the formal component of thought) are permeable and interrelated. The very conditions that make thought possible are echoed in our own instances of thinking.[16] *How* it is that we know is ever being revealed in the very act of knowing. Our path to thinking continually betrays what it is that makes thinking possible. It would be too onerous to explicate all of what is entailed in this for the task at hand, and yet a handful of comments are needed in order to make sense of what Schleiermacher has to say about space in *Dialectic* that will bear upon my reflections regarding place.

In the transcendental part of Schleiermacher's work (wherein he describes the condition for the possibility of thought), he expresses the heart of his argument in claiming that thinking is an instance of knowing and knowing contains the fullness of thought.[17] Knowing is the larger "category" encompassing thought. The reader is invited to imagine that thought is a more immediate and intentional activity focused on some contingent object, idea, or fact, while knowing is more broadly construed as the act of awareness that is ever present even while not yet thematized. The focused nature of thought—about this thing rather than all things—is made possible by knowing, which is attentive to all that is. The two together call us to attend to being:

> What is the object that is posited outside of thinking? When we think we are not only thinking but are thinking of something. What, then, is this something? Being. In every instance of thinking, what is thought is a knowing, what is known is a being. We cannot think except under the form of being, even if only in and for ourselves.[18]

Schleiermacher invites us to ponder "to think" as a verb that is always transitive in some fashion. We always think something and the thing we think is finally and fundamentally an instance of being. The mystery of life, its "is-ness," is manifest in every thought, from the mundane to the sublime and yet that is not all. Thinking aims at knowing and presumes reason as the human facility that enables the shared perceptions of what is.[19] Pure knowing is the awareness of all that is, of all that can be reasonably thought, and individual thoughts aim at instances of knowing that are true insofar as they coincide with what truly is. In sum, pure knowing is the sum of all knowledge that is manifest in particular instances of knowing that are achieved by the task of thought.

In a way, *Dialectics* is Schleiermacher's attempt to sketch out the relationship between the knower and the known.[20] Premodern thinkers were especially interested in this notion as a way to name that our knowing something or someone is of a piece with participating in their being—of considerable consequence for theology.[21] For both thinkers, thinking is not an exercise in "building castles in the sky" nor is it reducible to "just the facts." These would accord with the errors of idealism (what Schleiermacher calls "spiritualism") and mere empiricism (what he calls "materiality").[22] The art of philosophy needs to avoid these two ditches, and yet still recognize that ditches hold a truth in speaking to a limit of knowing. On the one hand, thought needs to accord with reality, and at the same time, thought needs to be reminded that reality ever speaks to the numinous, which can be neither thought nor felt in abstraction from the world and the relationship which constitutes it and puts us in its nexus. In sum, God cannot be directly perceived, nor deduced, but encountered in the world:

> What is absolute is not to be thought of as a singular thing that is exhausted only in an infinity of judgments; nor it is to be thought of as a concept caught

in the identity of a lower and a higher concept.... There is no such thing as an isolated perception of deity. Rather, we perceive the deity only in and with the collective system of perception. The deity is just as surely incomprehensible as the knowledge of it is the basis of all knowledge. Exactly the same is true also on the side of feeling.[23]

This quotation is important for three reasons. First, it establishes that we cannot know God empirically any more than we can know the sum of all knowable things. And yet, secondly, we *do* know God in the world in some fashion. We apprehend, or intuit, the totality of knowledge (pure knowing) in singular instances of thinking. Thirdly, this direct knowing of the singular that facilitates an indirect knowing of the whole speaks to the truth of feeling as a source for theological reflection. Yet, how does all of this bear upon the topic at hand: place? In the first instance it must be acknowledged that knowing presumes "the collective system of perception" (i.e., the senses in their totality) as the condition of possibility of knowing. Or, to put it another way, our senses help us so that we know sensually in space and time. Schleiermacher relates space to being and time to doing.[24] He identifies space as the outside-each-other of being. In other words, space is primarily the between-ness of two objects or agents. Such a between-ness, such a space is what makes a relationship possible. When space is negated, identity is achieved and the relationship is dissolved. I relate to my apple as an object only until the point at which I eat it, and then my relationship with it is mediated by memory—and so a different relationship obtains.

Schleiermacher's identification of space as the outside-each-other of being stands in stark contrast to time as the outside-each-other of doing. By contrasting being with doing, and identifying space as a "being" rather than "doing," Schleiermacher points us to space as the condition for the possibility of *receptivity*. We make space for the purpose of receiving what is needed. Yet receptivity for Schleiermacher is never about simple passivity. In *Christian Faith* he distinguishes passivity from a vibrant receptivity.[25] Receptivity includes an element of engagement. This affirms my subjectivity rather than reducing my being to being a mere object. Space is about a receptivity and attentiveness to what is, something of great importance to First Peoples, as is the balance between being and doing that is a part of the created order. This balance enabled them to apprehend all space and all places as sacred:

> Perhaps an outsider would describe the attitude of these Indians as one of awe or wonderment. We American Indians think of it as neither, but would prefer to call it respect, the appropriate attitude of respect necessary to fulfill our responsibility as part of the created whole, necessary to help maintain the harmony and balance, the interdependence and inter-relationship of all things in our world.[26]

It is interesting to note that this attentiveness to the whole draws to the fore a theme introduced in the first chapter: the distinction between space and place. Whereas space (the broader category containing place) points to the condition for the possibility of a relationship between entities, place points to the concretization of such a relationship. Place, therefore, is memorable. Yet, in a fashion, place serves as a portal for the arrival of space. With particular places we encounter possibilities realized, but beyond that we become aware of broader possibilities. Just as individual instances of thinking intimate our connection with pure knowing, so contingent places awaken us to the power of space and to the relationality of all that is.[27]

Reading Schleiermacher via an Indigenous attentiveness to place, then, allows us to see place as potent in opening us to the power of space, to consider that to which place points: space. To this end, place bears the sacred in harboring broader possibilities precisely because of its specificity, rather than in spite of this. The truth of the matter, for Schleiermacher, is that thought's specificity bears witness to awareness of universality. In like fashion, particular places point to space in all its fullness and give occasion for wonder. Yet, wonder well received ever advances in pursuit of the good. What, then, do we learn of place from the good?

PLACE AND THE GOOD

Schleiermacher's lectures on philosophical ethics have fallen under the critique of explicating a doctrine of the good in the mode of description rather than prescription.[28] Such a criticism, however, fails to understand the degree to which Schleiermacher's ethics builds upon his dialectic. Insofar as he advances the convertability of knowing and being, what we know engages us to the end that we are transformed by this knowing. We come to be with the object of our knowing and are shaped by it. To know what is, then, is not to succumb to the status quo since Schleiermacher proposes that we can know something of the highest good. To *know* the good is to be shaped by it. Here he parts from Kant, whom Schleiermacher critiques for presupposing a highest good rather than developing a doctrine of it.[29] Although he is, at one level, appreciative of Kant's project, which advances the notion of a categorical imperative, he fundamentally notes the need for a reversal of this as an ethic for modernity. Whereas the ancient world saw the good as primary and duty as secondary, Kant's work has reversed this order, which now itself needs a reversal.[30] Part of the task of advancing the good is to attend ethically to what is. In so doing, we have to understand that the word "ethic" for Schleiermacher is not about our individual inclinations. It is grounded in communal reason as an organism of virtue rather than a system of inclinations.[31]

Ethics, in sum, point to a humanity that has been formed socially under the tutelage of reason. It is important to underscore that for Schleiermacher, an ethic so formed implies sociality. He explored this at length in his 1812/13 lectures on philosophical ethics.

Schleiermacher's treatment of ethics in 1812/13 begins by outlining human community in four quadrants sketched by two fundamental data of human life: our modes of knowing and our modes of sociality. On the horizontal is sketched the universal and the particular and on the vertical is found the organizing (sometimes called the symbolizing, both of which point to the human interest in forming human community) and the cognizing (pointing to human interest in research, exploration, etc.). If one imagines a graph with universal left and particular right, and human organizing above cognizing the following quadrants—naming social phenomena—emerge in Schleiermacher's explication of human being (starting from the upper right corner and going clockwise): State (including the economic realm), Free Sociability (included here is the category of friendship), Church (included here is the arts as well), and Research Institute.[32]

Schleiermacher sketches society by imagining "places" that differently express our different modes of knowing and sociality. He locates ways of being human, and so invites us to imagine particular places where we will experience being human: the parliament, the salon, the art institute, the classroom. Being human, then, *takes place in places*. It should be recalled, of course, that Schleiermacher is outlining society in early 19th-century Berlin. For some it might be deemed a bit too neat, or formal. For others it might seem parochial in its choice of social groups. Where, for instance, would a meeting of the local anarchists fit in here? Or even labor unions? All told, these are important and fair critiques, but miss the significance of this phenomenology for the topic at hand: taking place seriously.

A way into the conversation might be illuminated by the work of Kahnawake Mohawk author Taiaiake Alfred, who recognizes a fundamental disconnect in how place is ordered in Western and Indigenous traditions:

> I think that "sovereignty" was a European word that tried to express the nationhood of a people who could think with one mind. Since the king was the ruler, he was sovereign in the sense that he was supposed to represent what the people of his nation wanted. Indians had spread out the idea of governing to include all the activities of life—thus, at times, medicine people would be influential and, at other times, warriors, or hunters, or scouts would be influential.[33]

Alfred describes different political imaginaries in exploring the distinction between European sovereignty and Indigenous nationhood. It is valuable to take this attentiveness to the distribution of power and engage it in

Schleiermacher's phenomenology of the ethical forms of state, free sociability, Church and the arts, and the university. Schleiermacher himself intimates a different way of viewing these social spaces: these four loci of human community inter-penetrate.[34] This more generally accords with Schleiermacher's understanding that two elements constituting a dialect are not diametrically opposed, but rather presume participation in each other.[35] Insofar as the spheres discussed by Schleiermacher are construed using two dialectical pairs, it can be presumed that free sociality does not exclude governance, nor does the academy preclude the arts or religion, etc. It seems, then, that Schleiermacher invites us to view social space in such a way that distinct spheres are not set over-against one another with impermeable boundaries carving out who goes where, any more than Indigenous societies structure their social orders in such a fashion that a frozen hierarchy obtains. In fact, Schleiermacher's ethic advances on the presupposition of an innermost unity of life.[36] Indeed, of a piece with Schleiermacher's ethics is the presumption that it is in connecting to the whole that makes any activity ethical.[37] Further to this, the highest good is construed in Schleiermacher's ethics as the organic unity of all goods rather than one, albeit supreme, good among all others.[38] We see, then, an intense attention to the whole in the thought of Schleiermacher, a point of emphasis that is well ensconced in the thought of the First Peoples of the Americas. Yet this attention to the whole is not meant to undercut the significance of the local. In speaking of the theme of "appropriation," which is used by Schleiermacher to speak of property ownership and the settlement of human community, he notes:

> Enter into each process of appropriation in such a way that you are already reconciled to it. . . . each people must appropriate on the soil where it has been put. The migration of whole peoples is an exception, and becomes increasingly impossible the more the process within the whole is underway according to this rule. Indeed it can only be justified when a people has somehow been cast out of its natural situation.[39]

Schleiermacher speaks against mass migrations since it makes it difficult to assert that "you're your place." While it might be necessary in extreme situations it certainly problematizes the mass migration of Europeans to the Americas resulting in the displacement of Indigenous Americans. And so Schleiermacher challenges us to ponder what it means to be in a place. He invites us to make peace with the place where we are, yet recognizing that having a place calls forth humans to act in the mode of hospitality.[40] Indigenous Americans have been fine exemplars of this, even though their hospitality has been returned with hostility. Yet the reason First Nations have been able to practice hospitality is because of their understanding of place, which presumes what Schleiermacher intimates in exploring the overlap of spheres, that is, that place is non-competitive.

What does it mean to advance the notion that place is non-competitive? In a sense, it upends much of the commonsense current among our contemporaries. Land deeds are declared to defend this piece of property as mine, and not yours. Property is deemed to be an extension of the body and so not susceptible to the claims of others. Indeed, this vision of place is the very thing that fueled the "Doctrine of Discovery," that insidious assumption that without deed, the Americas were vacant and so subject to expropriation.[41] By contrast, the First Nations of the Americas understood the land in such a fashion that it could not be owned.[42] It is hard to overstate the differences between these two views of land. Land is simply an instance of place, which is an instantiation of space. To pretend that one can own land is commonplace in settler sensibilities, and it is to assert the commodification of place and space. Yet, in some fundamental ways, this fiction is undone since I cannot refuse to pay taxes, and this demonstrates that others make legitimate claims on "my" property. Moreover, if the local government decides that a highway needs to be built through my neighborhood, I cannot willy-nilly circumvent this decision.

The fact is that we cannot own space, place, or land. It is not given to us; rather, it gives us the conditions for the possibility of life. We are gifted with a place to live and the First Nations of the Americas understood this truth, and so understood that land cannot be owned any more than one can own one's mother. The land is our mother and is finally hospitable to us in a way best exemplified by the loving mother who makes space and takes time for each of her children. Place is non-competitive insofar as competition is a fiction foisted on the earth, which Christians confess to be the Lord's.[43]

A non-competitive apprehension of space is simply a piece of a properly theological understanding of the stewardship of the earth. The earth hosts not only me and my generation, but those who preceded me and who will follow me. The earth takes the long view, and we are encouraged to do the same. There is finally and fundamentally a need to see what is true diachronically is also true synchronically. Others have claims on "my" property as surely as they do on my body—again this truth is borne out every time a country enacts a draft, or calls citizens to sit on a jury. The claim of others on me is of a piece with the unmasking of the fiction that I can own land. Theology asserts God alone as owner of anything, and God marks out the character of divine ownership by exhibiting generosity. Again, we cannot but compare and contrast Christian Europe's understanding of place with that of Indigenous Americans: the so-called "uncivilized natives" shamed Christians by their hospitable understanding of the nature of place. There is always room for more as long as we live together in a good way, that is, in harmony with the land, with one another, and with the Creator.[44]

Schleiermacher's treatment of truth speaks to us of the manner in which specific places host the fullness of space in such a manner that they open us to the wonder of being. His treatment of ethics, or the good, invited us in concert with insights from Indigenous Americans, to consider that place is non-competitive. What then can we learn from beauty, religion and art?

PLACE, RELIGION, AND ART

In what follows I will attend to one of Schleiermacher's most famous texts, *Speeches to the Cultured Despisers*.[45] From the outset, it should be noted that it is somewhat artificial to draw a simple line from the Greek emphases on truth, beauty, and goodness to Schleiermacher's texts on dialectics, ethics, and his *Speeches*. Schleiermacher did not set out to write three ripostes to Kant's Critiques, and in fact, his *Speeches* may be more properly considered in parallel with Kant's *Religion within the Limits of Reason*. Yet, there is a case for seeing the *Speeches* as treating the same themes as both the third critique and *Religion within the Limits of Reason*. In the *Speeches*, Schleiermacher observes, "Religion and art stand beside one another like two friendly souls whose inner affinity, whether or not they equally surmise it, is nevertheless still unknown to them."[46]

It is important to consider this quotation within the broader framework of the *Speeches*. In this work, Schleiermacher aims to draw unbelievers back into a religious conversation by first recognizing cultured critiques of religion—usually aimed at a somewhat rigid form of faith—as eminently sensible. He then distills from, or identifies something in, the critique that is religiously interested and reframes it in such a way that one of the essentials of Christian faith can be apprehended in a new key. The five chapters of the Speeches work through five themes: interiority as the province of religion, religion as redefined over-against metaphysics and morals, the impermissibility of proselytizing, the sociality of religion, and the relationship of Christianity to the religions. In each of these sections, imagination is the fundamental tool by which a re-construal of traditional categories is advanced.[47] Schleiermacher's attempts to reframe faith using imagination and intuition reflect his dual conviction that intuition and imagination allow us insights that are missed by arid propositionalism—and in fact are more faithful modes of apprehending religion, as well as his conviction that form and content are intimately connected. What, then, do we learn of place as we think about it while invoking the categories of beauty and religion?

From the outset, it is important to note that Schleiermacher sharply distinguishes the realm of religion from that of metaphysics and morals. This is a strategic distinction and invites the cultured despisers of religion to recognize that their refusal of many variants of religion is *a propos* in that too many theologians have allowed religion to become metaphysics or morality, and so have transgressed the religious intention, which enables us to intuit the whole in the particular.[48]

This theme of attending to the whole in the particular by way of intuition is also shared by art.[49] Art and religion both use intuition and imagination, yet Schleiermacher claims they part company in that art, by virtue of its medium, does not always have the universe—or the whole—as its object of wonderment, which is the case with religion.[50] In the exercise of attending to the particular in which the universal appears, the human subject oscillates between the small and great, the one and all, and in this oscillation experiences the phenomenon of the eternal.[51] Moreover, in this exercise of intuition, one becomes aware of the harmony of the universe evident in life's diversity. Schleiermacher writes:

> The magic *circle* of prevailing opinions and epidemic feelings encompasses and plays upon everything. Like an atmosphere filled with dissolving and magnetic forces, this *circle* fuses and unites everything. . . . That is the *harmony* of the universe, the wondrous and great unity in its eternal work of art.[52]

Indigenous Americans might find such a description of religious life as evocative and laudatory. The themes of harmony and circle are predominant in Indigenous thought, and are advanced in sharp contrast to what is deemed to be occidental fixation with progress.[53] The circle is taken by many to be a predominant metaphor for how to live; attentive to themes of renewal and return. Of especial interest is the manner in which the circle as the fundamental means by which to structure society admits the possibility of inclusion.[54] First Nations will often speak of widening the circle and prefer the circle to standard lecture hall formats for discussions, etc. I remember once sitting in a church meeting in a hall designed by the Cree architect Douglas Cardinal. We were discussing some especially contentious issues in a manner uncharacteristically irenic for that particular group, and one of the participants spoke to the fact that the architecture of the building softened our temperament. The curve of the place included all and invited a posture of reconciliation in our meeting. The circle bent us toward one another. This can perhaps be best illustrated by the story of the Cree chief Maskepetoon, who had been a warrior of renown but became known as a peacemaker in his conversion to Christianity:

> Years before, while the chief was away raiding, Blackfoot warriors had destroyed his camp, killing his aged father. Maskepetoon was told the name of his father's killer, but instead of pursuing revenge, he led his People into

the Beaver Hills for healing. He began to talk aloud about the wisdom of peace. Now, it was told, Cree warriors had brought several Blackfoot into Maskepetoon's camp and called out the name of the killer. The Blackfoot men were surrounded: the killer stood motionless facing the chief, waiting like a warrior for whatever would hit him.

Maskepetoon turned, went into his lodge, and emerged with his ceremonial warrior clothes, the suit of beads and quills and scalps he had not worn for years. Put this on, he said in Blackfoot, and after the man had done that he told him to mount the horse tied beside the lodge. Then Maskepetoon looked directly at him.

Both my hands are empty, he said. You took my father from me, so now I ask you to be my father. Wear my clothes, ride my horse, and when your People ask you how it is you are still alive, tell them it is because Maskepetoon has taken his revenge.

The Blackfoot warrior slid off the horse; he took Maskepetoon in his arms and held him hard against his heart.

My son, he said. You have killed me.[55]

This astounding narrative brings to the fore themes important to both Christianity and Indigenous spirituality: forgiveness, inclusion, peace, harmony, and reconciliation. Yet it holds, for me, a still more important learning in that this event took place a few kilometers from where I was born, which is now some 4,000 kilometers from where I live. In the process of writing this book, I spent some time on the Cree First Nation Maskwacis, which would have been the site of the above narrative and not far from the small farm I called home for the first 18 years of my life. In a way, this narrative is an invitation for me to make sense of the place I came from.

For youth, especially for those who have had the good fortune of having a stable home, young adulthood is a time of taking leave of a place. The place called home could more generally be identified as a launching pad, to which one rarely looks—or perhaps looks askance—in the adventure of life. Yet a story such as this helps me to experience a re-orientation to my place of origin. What was once a launching pad, in effect, becomes a landing pad; the locus of a return. This story brings me full circle. In a fundamental sense, we all need to come full circle and certain places make that possible. This story invites me to recognize anew how I am shaped by the place I knew as a child and youth; a place of both inclusion and discrimination; a place of both plenty and poverty; a place of misunderstanding, and yet a place that fed me with a curiosity that bred in me a desire to know more. Place matters at an existential level because it is both a repository for and a cipher of the formative people, events, and landscapes that shape our way of being in the world.

It seems that it is not only the case that we travel to or from a place, but that important places penetrate us. We are permeated with memories that are replete with significance, and every so often a visit to a significant place becomes a moment for pulling together what was disparate, or perhaps an opportunity to displace what has become an unhealthy fixation in our lives. Place can be a gift in such a sense; the opportunity to make whole what has been fractured. Schleiermacher used the word intuition to address that mode of knowing that attends to the whole. Noted Schleiermacher scholar Terrence Tice defines it as follows:

> For Schleiermacher, *Anschauung* [intuition] is indeed always a relatively internal phenomenon, because it is an internal mental function that registers what comes into the sensorium from relatively external sources, including the body. Nevertheless, the referent is always external relative to any given affective state.[56]

Tice goes on to note that this word can be variously used by Schleiermacher, and is often used to address the mundane, yet very important, phenomenon of sense perception. Yet Schleiermacher also chose to use this word in the phrase *Anschauung des Universums*,[57] to address a more profound intuition of the whole. What does this mean?

> He means a clear, straightforward apprehension of the universe as it is taken to be, in all its comprehensiveness. A patina of awe and wonder cling to the phrase, one such that perhaps no word in another language would bear a sound that would convey it, certainly not in English.[58]

It is instructive to note that Schleiermacher made use of a word that can have rather mundane uses in order to advance a sort of "experience" that awakens one to the Creator of all that is. Such a choice, by Schleiermacher, could certainly not be deemed to be accidental. This is because, like art, religion takes leave from the mundane to encounter the all before returning again to the mundane with a new purchase on reality. Place, even the simplest of places, can be such a launching pad, and a landing pad in turn. Place can awaken us to the harmony that intercepts our lives in those peculiar opportunities wherein they capture for us, what we seem to have lost on our own. Places can alert us to space as the condition for the possibility of the world that wraps us round. And particular places become imaginative markers that sustain us when we feel displaced. Places, in sum, become sacred sites when God transforms them by transforming us.

CONCLUSION

In setting Schleiermacher in conversation with Indigenous insights while exploring the theme of place, a few motifs came to the fore. We realized that particular places become profoundly potent in awakening us to the truth of space and the potency latent in it. Second, we explored the manner in which place is non-competitive, and so serves to alert us to the manner in which to have place is to be commended to the practice of hospitality and so to do the good. Third, we discovered how particular places can serve as a cipher for our apprehension of the beauty of the whole. It thereby serves as an occasion for our healing as we find ourselves ushered into a vision of the Reign of God wherein harmony is given to us as the sine qua non of that peace which provides sustenance in life. The kairotic space that occupies our interest, then, is characterized by not only a kenotic, but also a harmonic character.

Together, these three themes—the potency of place and space, the non-competitive nature of place, and the wholeness implicit in place—invite us to reflect further on the image of kairotic space as expansive and welcoming. In reflecting on Luther's theology, we imagine poetry as reflective of this roominess and so we consider next what it might mean to aver that kairotic space is poetic, too.

NOTES

1. See Friedrich Schleiermacher, *Christian Faith: A New Translation and Critical Edition*, eds. Terrence N. Tice, Catherine L. Kelsey, and Edwina Lawler (Louisville, KY: Westminster John Knox Press, 2016), 89, 90.

2. Kidwell et al., *Native American Theology*, 25.

3. George Lindbeck, *The Nature of Doctrine: Religious and Theology in a Postliberal Age* (Philadelphia, PA: The Westminster Press, 1984), 16.

4. Bruce Marshall, *Trinity and Truth* (Cambridge: Cambridge University Press, 2000), 51–54.

5. Allen G. Jorgenson, *The Appeal to Experience in the Christologies of Friedrich Schleiermacher and Karl Rahner* (New York: Peter Lang, 2007), 180.

6. Friedrich Schleiermacher, *On the* Glaubenslehre: *Two Letters to Dr. Lücke*, trans. James Duke and Francis Fiorenza (Chico, CA: Scholar's Press, 1981), 81.

7. Tinker, *American Indian Liberation*, 127: "As is the case in other liberation theologies, but in a significantly different sense, any American Indian articulation of theology will necessary be constructed on the foundation of experience." Of course varying theologians will differently go about this task of integrating experience, but its significance as an appeal for theology is categorically affirmed for the great majority of Indigenous thinkers.

8. Friedrich Schleiermacher, *On Religion: Speeches to the Cultured Despisers*, ed. and trans. Richard Crouter (Cambridge: Cambridge University Press, 1996), 123.

9. Julia A. Lamm, *The Living God: Schleiermacher's Theological Appropriation of Spinoza*, (University Park, PA: The Pennsylvania State University Press, 1996), 144–157.

10. Schleiermacher, *On the Doctrine of Election*, 73–79.

11. Woodley, *Shalom and the Community of Creation*.

12. See esp. Lamm, *The Living God*, 9.

13. Friedrich Schleiermacher, *Dialectics, or, the Art of Doing Philosophy: A Study Ed. Of the 1811 Notes*, trans. Terrence N. Tice (Atlanta: Scholars Press, 1998); *Lectures on Philosophical Ethics*, trans. Louise Adey Huish (Cambridge: Cambridge University Press, 2002); *Speeches* (see note 8 above); *Schleiermacher's Soliloquies*, trans. Horace Leland Friess (Chicago: Open Court, 1926). Cf also Hermann Peiter, *Christliche Ethik bei Schleiermacher—Christian Ethics according to Schleiermacher: Gesammelte Afsätze und Besprechungen—Collected Essays and Reviews*, ed. Terrence N. Tice (Eugene, OR: Wipf and Stock, 2010).

14. Schleiermacher, *Dialectics*, 7, 8.

15. Ibid., 5.

16. This is, in fact, related to his description of philosophy as an art. Art is a category more broadly deployed by Schleiermacher to point to the manner in which the universal is manifest in the particular.

17. Schleiermacher, *Dialectics*, 14.

18. Ibid., 16, 17.

19. Ibid., 17, 20, 21.

20. Aristotle, *On the Nature of the Soul*, trans. W. S. Hett (Harvard, MA: Harvard University Press, 1995), p. 165. In discussing the nature of thought Aristotle notes that the mind "must be potentially the same as its object, although not identical with it."

21. And so, Schleiermacher was concerned that certain Lutheran theologians divorced God's declaring us righteous from God's making us righteous. See *Reformed but Ever Reforming: Sermons in Relation to the Celebration of the Handing Over of the Augsburg Confession (1830)*, trans. Iain G. Nicol (Lewiston: The Edwin Mellen Press, 1997), 70.

22. Schleiermacher, *Dialectics*, 39.

23. Ibid., 31.

24. Ibid., 46. "Space is the outside-each-other of being, time the outside-each-other of doing. Inner space or filled space represents the manifold of a thing in the unity of its being. Every filled space represents an inner contrast; where this contrast ceases, as does that between soul and body, there is also no spatial relationship there. Every intermediate space represents an external contrast, where this contrast ceases as occurs with the world overall, there is also no intermediate space there. Action negates space. Two agents are immediately present to each other." Schleiermacher's use of "contrast" here invites the thinker to think of relationality: or we could say "over-against-ness." Inner space speaks to those perfect instances wherein what is over-against is unified. Here he uses the example of the body and soul. Intermediate

space—that is, space amid (inter) the middle (*medius*)—speaks to those instances wherein two objects relate in a tension sustained by time until action negates the tension.

25. Schleiermacher, *Christian Faith*, 559.
26. Kidwell et al., *Native American Theology*, 33, 35.
27. See 1 Cor. 13:12 "Now I know in part, then I shall know fully, even as I have been fully known."
28. Robert B. Louden, "Introduction," in Friedrich Schleiermacher's *Lectures on Philosophical Ethics*, xxx.
29. Schleiermacher, *Lectures on Philosophical Ethics*, 4.
30. Ibid., 11.
31. Ibid., 12.
32. Ibid., 13–25.
33. Alfred, *Peace, Power, Righteousness*, 90, 91.
34. See Schleiermacher, *Ethics*, 43: "In reality, therefore, these areas are not at all separate; for when one makes an object of either quantity in itself or absolute unity in itself, the task can only be resolved by means of a series of individual actions, in which there is immediately an element of reality, and so it acquires a share in what is opposed to it." See also Ibid., 25.
35. Schleiermacher, *Dialectics*, 6.
36. Schleiermacher, *Lectures on Philosophical Ethics*, 180.
37. Ibid., 29.
38. Ibid., 163.
39. Ibid., 235.
40. Ibid., 233.
41. See Jennifer Reid, "The Doctrine of Discovery and Canadian Law," *Canadian Journal of Native Studies* 30, no. 3 (2010): 335–359. See also Allen Jorgenson, "Immigrants as *Terra Nullius*: On the Need for a Comparative Theology of Decolonization," in *The Meaning of My Neighbor's Faith,* eds. Alexander Y. Hwang and Laura E. Alexander (Lanham, MD: Lexington Books/Fortress Press, 2019).
42. Harold Cardinal, "First Nations sovereignty and Native Liberation: Okimaw Win and Post-Colonial Nation-Building," in *Intersecting Voices*, 195.
43. Psalm 24:1.
44. Woodley, *Shalom and the Community of Creation*, 21.
45. Op. cit. This text played such an important role in the development of theology in the early 19th century in that it was an instance of a theological apologetics addressing Enlightenment by leveraging romanticism in concert with certain themes in Christianity. The fact that Schleiermacher returned to this text and reproduced it two more times, making three versions available to students of Schleiermacher, speaks to both his conviction of its importance in the development of this thought as well as its role in the intellectual currents of the day,
46. Schleiermacher, *Speeches*, 69.
47. A similar project is attempted in *Soliloquies* using the five categories of reflection, soundings, world, prospect, youth, and age in *Soliliquies*.

48. Schleiermacher, *Speeches,* 24, 25. "I entreat you to become familiar with this concept: intuition of the universe. It is the hinge of my whole speech; it is the highest and most universal formula of religion on the basis of which you should be able to find every place in religion, from which you may determine its essence and its limits. . . . Thus to accept everything individual as a part of the whole and everything limited as a representation of the infinite is religion."

49. Schleiermacher, *Dialectics*, 4.

50. Schleiermacher, *Speeches*, 24–26.

51. Ibid., 43.

52. Ibid., 40, 41. Emphases mine.

53. Woodley, *Shalom and the Community of Creation*, 96–100.

54. John Ralston Saul, *A Fair Country: Telling Truths About Canada* (Toronto: Viking Canada, 2008).

55. Wiebe, *Big Bear*, 24, 25.

56. Terrence Tice, *Abingdon Pillars of Theology: Schleiermacher* (Nashville, TN: Abingdon Press, 2006), 23, 24.

57. "Intuition of the universe."

58. Tice, *Schleiermacher*, 25.

Chapter 4

The Poetic Potency of Place

RECAPITULATION

In our journey to the theme of place thus far, we have been tutored by voices Indigenous to North America, as well as those of Luther and Schleiermacher. The former invited us to imagine the importance of land, place, and space as we think through what it means to be authentic in this land called Turtle Island by some of North America's First Nations. The poet reminds us:

We were the land before we were people,
loamy roamers rising, so the stories go,
or formed of clay, spit into with breath reeking soul—[1]

Indigenous voices have spoken of the need to attend to the importance of place, to harmony as our way of being, and to let the circle rather than the timeline set in the mode of trajectory to guide our way. We have been invited to begin with community.

As I have carried these lessons into my reading of Luther and Schleiermacher, new themes have come to the fore for me. From Luther, we have been invited to see creation as a peer of redemption, and to understand the *Spiritus Creator* as the poetic force who enables us to experience the kenotic God in kairotic places. From Schleiermacher we noted the potency of seeing how place opens us to the breadth of space, the non-competitive nature of place, and the harmonic wholeness implicit in place. In what follows, I will engage this grounded attention to place to imagine a poetically rich engagement of ways to take place seriously, in part by thinking it playfully to the end that we can discern *kairotic* places. So, we begin with poetry.

Chapter 4

INDIRECT DISCOURSE, INDIRECT PLACE

Soundings

The ground we kept our ear to for so long
Is flayed or calloused, and its entrails
Tented by an impious augury
Our island is full of comfortless noises.[2]

The poet speaks from his native Ireland, and yet there is a tone here that sounds across continents. Ground everywhere suffers human violence. Yet, what portends our future when we no longer have a memory of keeping our ear to the ground? What possibility lay in a human community wherein even those attentive to revelation, to transcendence, to possibilities not yet unearthed no longer dream of earth's potency? Where will we find hope for a future in a human community too proud to put its knees to the ground, much less its ears?

It is easier and cheaper to despair than to hope, and yet the clarion call of the gospel is a sound of hope in times of hopelessness; a call to fall in faith, all the while remembering those times in which fall was not a fear but a delight—those halcyon days of childhood, of unquestioning faith, days of dreaming. The gospel invites us to fall and even to fail, because failure follows play, the ridiculous, and so it is the arrival of a freedom: a kind of freedom not opposed to necessity but resting in the necessity of freedom, and necessarily teaching us that comfortless noises can no longer be avoided. Yet even this hard truth is truth, and truth leads to freedom. But what is freedom, and how can it comfort ears seared with "comfortless noises"? Freedom is variously construed. Luther's treatise on Christian freedom frames our answer to the question in this context:

A Christian is a perfectly free Lord of all, subject to none,
A Christian is a perfectly dutiful servant of all, subject to all.[3]

Freedom takes place, then, in between these two truths. We know these two to be true, even when we refuse the claims of one or the other or both. These claims come to us in our dealings with people and our environment. Perhaps one or the other forces itself first on us: in this instance I find my relationships with those nearest to me binding me in a kind of happy necessity. I cannot be here, because my child needs to be there. I cannot sleep because diapers need changing. I cannot attend this concert because the dying need attending.

Our relationships bind us in a way that frames our life by a seeming necessity that sometimes seems burdensome: but no, that is not quite right. Or if it is, it is by a re-construal of burden. Yes, these are burdens, but burdens with a difference. Burdens that locate me in relationship and allow me to be, not by erasure of freedom but by carving a space in which freedom can finally and fully come to be. Freedom, in this framing, is rather like poetry. Poetry arrives not by the erasure of grammar, but rather by grammar's form and functionality. Grammar speaks to limits, yet only by hinting at the play of the limit. Limit is the place where the center is reconceived, where the hold of the whole is given its contours, its shape. A happy accident occurs at the near coincidence of the English word for place and the Latin word for please: *placeo*. Place sounds pleasure: that is, it provides a sounding for pleasure, a measure wherein we discover the freedom that comes from having space carved out for Christian freedom. Is not this the message of the cross?

The cross is the narrative center of the Christian life but not first as a symbol of the human sin that sacrifices our savior; not first as a marker of our need to unwillingly and unwittingly unburden ourselves of the future by an unchecked and chequered servitude to suffering. No—the cross does not only serve to sound the certainty of death in the human experience, but also the depth of divine accompaniment to our choral strains. God, yes God in Christ, dies with us, not as a lament for human frailty and failure but as a *Grundton* for our singing of life. The cross marks God's place in our life at death, but not death simply as a kind of punishment (although that too obtains in a certain fashion), but death as the conditions for the possibility of life. Life is lived over against death because death makes space and takes place for life. This is manifestly evident whenever we eat. As Ojibwe author Basil Johnston reminds us, we live by another's death.[4] Death inscribes life, and the divine death inscribes the divine life as accompaniment. God holds the center and edge so that we can play in between, so that we can find pleasure "in the midst of," so that we can find the place that pleases us by freeing us to live, not only in fear of death, but in thanks to death. Yes, we can, in all things give thanks (Phil 4:4), because death is God's circumscription of our being that shocks us into the joy of life (Heidegger). The Christian who moves along with Plato also moves beyond the Greek, by being shocked not at creation alone, but also by re-creation. Doubly shocked and so doubly blessed. Or so it would seem, but this does not seem to be manifestly true. Why is this?

We return again to the cross. The cross not only marks God's being with us at death and so life, but it also speaks that deep and dark truth of our refusal to accept it to be so. Why? Because we continually desire to make God into our image, and death is not our aspiration and yet God in Christ dies. We aspire not to die, presuming a way of living that is not grounded in the truth of death. Yet language betrays the truth we refuse: To aspire (ad-spirare) is to breathe, or blow, *toward* and the primordial instance of aspiration for the human paradigm in the Christian tradition is Christ's last breath from the cross as he "gives up the ghost" (KJV). This is precisely what we refuse: the dying of Christ because that dying means my dying, and dying is finally nothing other than my loss of control. Death is finally a given, something that I cannot control.[5] Death is a given—and even a giving—yet not always a giving as we wish. We all want to die a good death, but death isn't always good, and so Luther's insistent and constant narration of human consternation as being plagued by "sin, death and the devil" rings true. Death is the middle term in this frequent phrase. Death splits the difference between the individuality of human sin and communal evil's personification in the wily serpent. The individual and the community share death's denial of truth. Yet all three instances—individual sin, death, and communal evil—are parasitic on their healthy counter truths. Life is the negotiation between the individual and the communal in a fashion that *always means a dying. This* possibility always becomes actual rather than *that* possibility. Something is always given up in order that something else can be. Life is the play of these possibilities. Life takes place in the inter-play of these possibilities. Above all else, life *takes place*. This is true in two senses. First, life happens before our beckoning it. Second, when life happens it does so in the play of place and so to live authentically we need to live attentive to place and the play of place. Perhaps it is best to begin the second, because for too many of us, place has not really been in play for a long time.

Meet your Mother

> It's no metaphor to feel the influence of the dead in the world, just as it's no metaphor to hear the radiocarbon chronometer, the Geiger counter amplifying the faint breathing of rock, fifty thousand years old. (Like the faint thump from behind the womb wall.) It is no metaphor to witness the astonishing fidelity of minerals magnetized, even after hundreds of millions of years, pointing to the magnetic pole, minerals that have never forgotten magma whose cooling off has left them forever desirous. We long for place; but place itself longs. Human memory is encoded in air currents and river sediment. Eskers of ash wait to be scooped up, lives reconstituted.[6]

The novelist Anne Michaels invites us into a different world, but not a world different by its strangeness so much as by its un-confronted familiarity. That place yearns is, as she notes, no metaphor but rather a deep abiding truth and, as per the disposition of deep truth, the yearning of place is a suppressed truth. But what do I mean by that?

In the first instance, this truth is only unearthed (or perhaps "earthed" if you will), by seeing the same world we live in via different eyes. For North Americans, an important set of eyes to behold is that of the First Nations of this continent. They see the world differently, some might say that they see it ab-originally—from the perspective of those originally here: not as visitors, or immigrants, or transplants to a place anew to them, but rather as rooted inhabitants who have a sense for this place in their DNA—that is, born and bred into them. So, what might we learn from Indigenous North Americans? I have already listed and encountered some important truths: the importance of the land for the religious imagination; the role of harmony and balance for human and ecological flourishing; the possibilities inherent in the idea of beginning with community; and the role of story in the genesis of a people. There is another important theme, one that distinguishes Indigenous from Western thought (more generally conceived) that we have not yet broached, and this theme first became clear for me in my encounters with First Nations through stories of the origin of hunting. Many Indigenous accounts chronicle the manner in which various species confer with one another as to the need for the human species—late comers to Mother Earth—to have food to eat and offer their own species for that purpose. Much can be made of that image, and more will be in the last section of this chapter; but the theme that especially interests me at this juncture in our journey is the way in which occidental sensibilities are confronted by the rather unbiblical image of the animals deciding to offer themselves to us, rather than animals being offered to us by God.[7] At this point in the larger Indigenous narrative, a fissure between our stories seems to emerge. In the Indigenous narrative humans are not the only sentient beings. Animals are considered brothers and sisters, but not animals alone. Stones, as noted above, are considered "grandfathers," who in the sweat lodge, are given voice.[8] These oldest members of the living community have something to say for those with Indigenous sensibilities. The yearning of place is no metaphor for the eldest of the North American peoples. Yet what might this mean for Christians? Is the telling of the tale of talking stones a cute picture, or an antiquated image, or fodder for the mill of demytholigizing? A detour in method is in the offing.

The emerging discipline of comparative theology recognizes that North Americans have much to learn from religions and cultures the world over, cultures in which the great religions have emerged side by side. These places have certainly seen that differing religious worldviews can, in the wrong instances, lead to untold strife in the human community and betrayal of the shared desire to see our life together flourish. But at its best, the coexistence of differing religions has potential for each and for all religions insofar as they accept the other as a gift. This is, of course, as astoundingly difficult to do as it is easy to say. Yet, for Christians, there is within the tradition more broadly conceived resources for thinking about the religions in this vein. In a theology of creation, we are invited to ponder the giftedness of all that is, and all that is, is diverse. Diversity is the *sine qua non* of creation. Scientists witness to the importance of biodiversity as the condition for the possibility of the flourishing of the environment. Social scientists, artists, and thinkers of various stripes have witnessed the incredible wealth of creativity when human communities with varied traditions, histories, and sensibilities find a way to emerge in communities of difference that share enough commonality to advance the causes of healing for the cosmos and peace among peoples. North America is sometimes seen as an experiment in the power of difference as peoples from the world over converge into a microcosm of the gift of diversity. Yet, this experiment has gone awry in the totalizing project of mainstream North America, with its mania for efficiency that fuels standardization.

The human condition is such that our propensity for stifling difference with sameness is quickly built into our processes such that the factory becomes the grand metaphor for how to structure social well-being. Whatever generates the most profit with the least labor costs is deemed the wisest. Yet, we know that this cannot be so. There is a profound life-transforming genesis that occurs when differences are allowed to emerge. There is something profoundly sensible in the so-called postmodern embrace of alterity. Yet as many scholars note, postmodernity, is not so very far removed from modernity and its propensity for flattening difference by demanding social performances that nod toward difference while expecting compliance in the social sphere, often deemed secular. How might theology, and a comparative theology in particular, help in this situation?

Some scholars of comparative theology work under the assumption that interreligious encounter is a gift for many reasons, part of which is knowing the neighbor is fundamental to the tasks of healing the planet and promoting peace. This seems fundamental. Yet others also underscore that the experience of encountering the other allows one to know the self in new ways. In point of fact, the case might be made that it is impossible to know the self without knowing the other, who allows me to come to myself in deeper ways with a more penetrating analysis. And so we might ask, what has all of this to do with the task at hand, with pondering the play of place in our religious imaginations?

If a cross-religious encounter is a gift, how does it unwrap our sense of self? Simply by allowing us to return to the self with new eyes, attentive to who we are. Simon Weil has written that "attention is the rarest and purest form of generosity."[9] Weil points us to attention in construing the ethical task because ethics and epistemology never function discretely. How we care for the other and how we know the self are shared tasks, sharing tools of the trade. We care for the other by attending to the other, and we know the self more attentively in so doing. When we pay attention to what the other offers—despite, or perhaps because of, its seeming otherness—we discover the otherness of our own position, and sometimes that means we see in ourselves what was "other." I think this is most manifestly the case as we think about place in Christianity.

Christians in many and various ways have privileged *Homo sapiens*, using a variety of biblical passages to do so. The human is given "dominion" over creation. The human alone is deemed to be made in the image of God. God in Christ came to save sinners, and since humans alone sin, the incarnation was an event for the human community alone.[10] There are various ways in which the common parlance of theology renders humans as the actors on the stage of creation. Yet is this the truth of the Bible? This is manifestly not the case! The psalmist declares:

Praise the Lord from the earth
You sea monsters and all deeps
Fire and hail, snow and frost
Stormy wind, fulfilling his command! Psalm 148: 7–8

In the psalms we also hear of the mountains bearing witness as the Lord holds court. There are donkeys that talk in the Hebrew scriptures. God has intimate knowledge of sparrows in the discourse of Jesus. Paul writes to us that creation groans. This latter is perhaps the most poignant both in giving the cosmos voice, and in allowing us to hear the content of that cry: "for freedom from its bondage to decay and [that it] will obtain the freedom of the glory of the children of God" (Rom. 8:21).

Creation is giving birth and as it does it cries like any mother, yearning for its freedom from the travails of birth and for freedom for its children. It is most important to underscore that Paul does not picture the cosmos *as if* it were a mother bearing birth, but rather Paul pictures the earth *as* a mother bearing birth: no "if" is countenanced here. This is not a metaphor: this is a fundamental cosmic truth. Creation is in pain, labor pain, and she cries. The world yearns for newness; yearns for deliverance; yearns for freedom. To make of this a metaphor is to romanticize somatic sensibilities; it is to make of the body a vehicle for the soul; to make of the other a tool for the self and creation fodder for the human. This latter is most insidious in its being a matricide. There is something profoundly life giving in the Indigenous narrative that hears creatures choose to give themselves to the human community so that the human community might flourish and, in turn, give back to the end that both human and nonhuman communities flourish. The trajectory of thought that moves from Romans 8:21 to Big Box Ecclesiology baffles the imagination. Yet First Nations communities, with their attentiveness to the gift of the land and their intuitive attention to the land as maternal, invite us to reimagine the ways in which place yearns and as such plays on our imagination. A theology of place recalls, then, that theology is rooted in the land, which is marked with fingerprints of the Creator, a point often forgotten by contemporary Western Christians. Indigenous cultures have kept manifest what has often become latent to occidental sensibilities, even while the history of pilgrimages in the Christian tradition were attentive to the power of place. It is now given to us to imagine and to dream what takes place when place itself is given voice anew. What happens in the hearing of place?

Ambiguous Gains

The sun is scorching. The plane comes in low,
Throwing a shadow in the shape of a giant cross, rushing over
   The ground.
A man crouches over something in the field.
The shadow reaches him.
For a split-second he is in the middle of the cross.
I have seen the cross that hangs from the cool church arches.
Sometimes it seems like a snapshot
of frenzy.[11]

Life takes place. Life happens. Frenzy. The poet notes that sometimes it is in "cool church arches" that the chaos of life comes clean. Sometimes it is in the Sabbath that we finally and fully take hold of mess the life that is; life messed up with death. Death in the cross-sections of life is often the condition for the possibility of seeing the arrival of life. But because death and life take place, they require place, some*place* for this arrival, for this revelation to revolve our seeing of the world. What is this place that allows us to see in a new way? In the Christian tradition we speak of the arrival of seeing as follows:

> From now on, therefore, we regard no one from a human point of view, even though we once knew Christ from a human point of view, we know him no longer in that way. So if anyone is in Christ, there is a new creation: everything old has passed away; see everything has become new! (2 Cor. 5:16–17)

In the Greek text, the last sentence literally reads, "So if anyone in Christ, creation new. The old things have passed away. Behold they have become new!" Two points bear upon our consideration of this text for pondering the play of place. First, it is to be noted that, unlike older translations of this text, the NRSV renders more clearly the manner in which the passage allows us to understand that it is not only the human who is a new creation in Christ, but creation itself is new. Second, for the one who sees everything new, they do so because they see Christ anew because they see *from* Christ. We begin by pondering this second consideration.

Paul notes that we used to see Christ according to the flesh (*kata sarka*), but this is no longer the case. And the reason this is no longer the case is because our locus for seeing has been changed, we see *in Christ*. It is not so much the case that our eyes have been changed (although that too is true), but rather that we see from a new locale, that of being in Christ. Christ is where we are, where we take place, and as a result of that everything that we once regarded as the old things (*ta archaia*) have become new. Old things, here, has phonetic resonance with the word for foundation (*arche*) and so invites to consider the word more broadly in terms of foundations, or, things well established. For modern readers with a propensity for novelty, the term "old" strikes us as pejorative. This need not be the case here. Even those things known from the beginning—the established things—have become new because they are seen from a new place, that of being in Christ, which suggests that we now see with Christ's eyes. Kairotic moments gain toeholds. Cool church arches render life in a new key. The cross is no longer an image for sacred pious reflection, but becomes transformed into a cipher for frenzy, yet not frenzy as chaos (although that too is true in a certain sense), but rather the ebullience of life, the bubbling, expressive power of life that recognizes death as the plane crosses the vision of the poet. He is invited to cross himself in the remembrance of death, because life happens at the edge of human existence. This kairotic frenzy is edgy. Kairotic places are at the edge. Life boils over at the moment of dying, and yet for those with eyes to see and ears to hear—in Christian parlance, for those in Christ—death is an existential of life. We always live at the edge when we are in Christ because we are ever where Christ is, with the marginalized, on the cross, even in the very halls of hell (as per the creed). Christ is ever on the edge, because the edge is where life is experienced kairotically.

Pondering place in Christ invites us to the edge, to the limits of human existence, and the contour of the limit is the cross. Cross is the epistemological entry point for our seeing in Christ. We enter Christ crucified, in both senses of the word. We enter the crucified Christ, and we enter him by being crucified, dying in baptism to live in the crucified and resurrected Christ. And from that vantage point we see that creation is new. The world is seen in a new light. We see differently, because we see the cross as it shadows the man crouching over something in the field. The frenzied possibilities of that rather quotidian activity becomes a new possibility for those who see with the pupils of pupils. We are being schooled in life by being thrust in death.

Death becomes us, in the sense that we no longer live simply afraid of death, but expectant of death. Death enables us because death is the condition for the possibility of life. To some extent we have already been over that in the text above, but now it is time to ponder what that means as we think about place. The place of death in our thinking can only be retrieved by remembering that we have experienced something of a death of place in our thinking. Vine Deloria Jr has clearly articulated the dying of place in the occidental mind by recounting the ascent of time in Western sensibilities. Yet, I suggest, it need not be so. Christians find a way to re-place our thinking: in Christ. In Christ, we see the world anew: creation has become new, but Paul could not have imagined a world in which place was second to time (nor the reverse for that matter). The typically modern way of reading eschatology offers us a case in point. We generally read eschatological texts as if the referent of the *eschatos* was utterly temporal.[12] Yet this need not be the case alone. *Eschatos* can reference place and order as well. The last things are not only the last things but can also be the things at the edge. Thinking place invites to the edge of life, where death and life meet in the symbiosis that establishes the condition for the possibility of flourishing. Yet eschatology is not the only doctrine that can be reclaimed spatially. The renewal of first things, or foundational things, invites us to think about the doctrine of creation anew.

The doctrine of creation has become problematic in Christianity. The reformation *solae* have too often had the unintended effect of fixing the Protestant imagination on the doctrine of redemption.[13] While there is nothing wrong with being attentive to the doctrine of redemption, there is a need for Christians to see with two eyes, that is, an eye on redemption at the same time as having an eye on creation. The doctrine of creation has been muted by many things, but perhaps nothing has so muted it in the Protestant imagination (and here I suspect we have shared our propensities with our Catholic brothers and sisters even while our Orthodox kindred have been cautious in accepting this Trojan horse) as our need to make sense of evil by making it sensible. The tautological edge of this last sentence is intended and can be bolstered by some insights from Indigenous thinkers.

In Indigenous creation stories, there is no exodus from Eden. Humans are not born in original sin. They are born on the land, and from the hand of the Creator they receive the instructions for leading life in communion with all and in harmony with the place in which they have been put. If they fail in their relationships, there are means by which the balance can be restored, and they are able to die at harmony with the cosmos. As noted above: we are born whole, we stay whole by walking in the right way and so we die whole. This construal does not deny the problems we face in life, nor does it propose that evil does not exist. Anyone who has dealt with the stigmatization and marginalization of First Nation communities knows too well the reality of evil. Yet the propensity for telling the whence of evil is problematized by locating it in characters, such as the Trickster, who are far more ambiguous than the snake of Genesis 3. Good and bad both come from the Trickster, and from other cosmic characters.[14] Evil cannot be explained, but rather dealt with, by attention to the harmonic possibilities of creation. By attending to the land and its tales, people experience what is needed to endure evil and even thrive in community. But how might this help Christian discourse?

I certainly do not want to undo Christian discourse around evil, but rather what I suspect is needed is a way of reading our foundational stories that makes the appearance of evil more ambiguous and so truer to its genesis, and Genesis. To begin with, we need to recognize that Genesis 3 is not the only tale of evil's genesis. If we work with a doctrine of creation that presumes that creation is an eternal event, always happening, then an evil parasitic upon creation is continually coming into being. The whole Bible is a tale of sin's "genesis." Moreover, sin and evil often seem, in some aspect, to be occluded by the fact that sometimes a gain (legitimate or not) in life accompanies the losses demanded by sin, death, and the devil. In the scorching heat, the cross comes as a shadow. The instrument of torture comes in the guise of respite. Yet the affronting truth of this is that while sometimes some sort of a gain has actually been achieved, the cost has been horrific. Some children really did learn to read, write, and do mathematics in residential schools even while that can never excuse the hell experienced by residential school students. But that is the nature of evil: most often cloaked in ambiguity and then rendering ambiguity itself as anathema. But First Nations insights affirm the best of Christian thought in reminding us that at the edge where death and life meet, ambiguity is unavoidable. The gain of a meal is the loss of a life. The loss of the old things is the gain of a new creation. We tend not to mourn the old things that have passed away, but why not? If the old things were made by God, if they were they were at some level good by the grace of creation, then what they were insofar as their being depended upon God is to be mourned in their passing away. Even if the birth of a new self is freedom from bondage to sin, death, and the devil, then the death of that old self is to be mourned, not as an affirmation of that bondage, but as a recognition that those in bondage are deserving of respect.[15] When someone dies to be in Christ, a loss is registered even while the new birth is a gain. It is important that we recognize that our life before Christ was not *as nothing*: it was a crouching in a scorching field, and whereever human life etches out an existence, there is God. New creation is only possible where there has been creation, and where there has been creation there has been good, and insofar as anything that is good has been lost, even if for the sake of the better, mourning its loss is an appropriate response. The cross *always* is an ambiguous symbol pointing both to the tragic death of the beloved and the hope that is engendered as God brings life from death as life takes place by taking the place of death—and in the instance of Christ—death takes place by taking the place of life. Again, a gain sustained by a loss.

The Place of Play and the Play of Place

> To the august and honorable Hans Löser, hereditary marshal of Saxony, my gracious lord and dear friend.
>
> GRACE and peace in Christ, my august, honorable, and dear lord and friend:
>
> When I was with you recently, trying to drive away the buzzing and weariness of my head through physical exercise, you showed me the honor and kindness

of taking me along on a hunting trip. At the same time I did some spiritual hunting on my own as I sat in the carriage; I bagged Psalm 147, *Lauda Jerusalem*, together with its exposition, and this was my happiest hunt and grandest game. Now that I have brought it home and carved it, I want to tell you about it, lest I have a bad conscience for having concealed a prize won on your estate and be found ungrateful and destructive. I am sending Your Honor the whole thing, and yet I am keeping all of it for myself. This kind of game can be shared among friends in such a wonderful way that everyone gets all of it while no one comes short. May it please Your Honor to accept it, for I am glad to serve you.

God be with you and with your vine and olive plants! Amen.

Saturday after St. Lucy's, 1531. DR. MARTIN LUTHER[16]

Luther is not generally thought of as a poet, yet his deep love of the psalms, his hymn writing, and the above quotation reveal a poetic sensibility in him. It is an astounding thing for us to imagine "bagging" a psalm! And yet there is something profoundly helpful about this image, both in and of itself, and also as we deploy Luther's use of the same in offering it to "his gracious Lord and dear friend." First, then, what does it mean to "bag" a psalm?

Luther invites us to imagine exegesis with an eye to hunting. This ought to give us pause, and pause is nothing other than space, both space in time and space in place. Pause arrests us by disallowing us to move in the direction we had intended. At first blush, this can be annoying. Who wants to be arrested? Yet this moment of suspension allows the mind to savor the event of being turned upside down by a wordplay, by an image, by the luxurious sound of language that allows us to see the world anew by making us new. Luther's image, here, in concert with the *opera* of poets and their disciples, locates a Sabbath, or a seventh, for us. What might this mean for our pondering place?

As noted above, place can quite simply be the geographical analogue to rest: a point played out in the expression "to make space." It is the opening of a *locus* that allows us to suspend our activity, to let our burden down for a time, to remember why we exist, and for whom we exist. Place is pause in geography with the same kind of possibility we find inherent in a space in a piece of music. It creates the conditions for the possibility of hearing the notes and accords us the sensibilities to rejoice, to play. Luther considered joy the deep gift that comes to us from the gift of music.[17] Yet joy is not all that music (complete with temporal space) and room (as the gift of geographic space) allow; space in time and place allows us to imagine that play and work are ordered to one another. Place, in sum, gives us the breathing room for apprehending that cessation and engagement are parasitic upon one another. Luther's appeal to the hunting metaphor allows us to ponder this truth more deeply. How so?

In the first instance, Luther's appeal to hunting here is set over against the "weariness and buzzing in his head," or to put the matter differently, the drudge of work. Hunting for a "hereditary marshall" is play, a relaxing diversion. It is a sport. Yet what is sport?

In the time I served as a Pastor in a Northern community in Alberta, my wife volunteered as Vice President for the Arctic Winter Games that were hosted by our community in Slave Lake, Alberta. I learned something about the north in this event, attended by peoples who live north of the 55th parallel. I was especially intrigued by the Inuit games. These games, foreign to many southerners, were developed over the centuries of Innu existence in the far north. They were a way to do two related things: they provided distraction during the long winter months as well as allowed Innu hunters to keep hunting skills sharp in all seasons of the year. For this reason, play is an important, a very important activity in the life of human community, and around the place of play, human community more deeply forms to the end that relationships are developed and skills sharpened that allow community to continue to exist. Moreover, as Luther's example shows us, the boundary between play and work is porous and invites us to reconsider how we conceive of the relationship between the two.

Just as Innu winter games sharped skills for hunting, so the grand Marshall's hunt provides food for the table; and in the same way that hunting is a sport and a means for the procurement of life-sustaining food *at the same time*, Luther's playful pondering of the task of exegesis accords us similar insights. He bags "Psalm 147" as he waits in the carriage. No sport with bow and arrow for him. No, Luther leisurely waits out the hunt in the princely carriage, but it is in this place, circumscribed by the relative luxuries of distance from the demands of quotidian existence, that a new kind of work arrives: a meditation on Psalm 147 in a new key. This psalm itself kindly speaks of the God who builds up a broken people and identifies this God with the God who "covers the heavens with clouds" (verse 8) to the end that rain refreshes all so that grass grows to feed animals and birds (verse 9). This same God grants peace as surely as snow (verses 14–16); he sends word as he does the wind (verse 18). We almost have the impression from this that God plays; that the world itself is something of a playground for God; and if God is pictured as "taking pleasure in those who fear him" (verse 11), then pleasure itself is sanctified and places of pleasure are accorded a measure of respectability that we otherwise might not imagine. All the world is the place of God's pleasure. Moreover, when places of pleasure are thereby sanctified, place itself is seen anew. Place is deemed to be the condition for the possibility of the arrival of the gifts of God. There is no hunting without game lands. There is no exegesis without texts. Place allows play to emerge as both Luther and the Marshall do what gives them the greatest pleasure, but Luther finds a great joy not only in what he bags, but in what he is able to do with what is bagged.

Luther notes, "This kind of game can be shared among friends in such a wonderful way that everyone gets all of it while no one comes short."[18] Of course, that is the nature of "game" in both senses of the word. "Game," as in "sport" really only exists by sharing the activity of play with the other. Likewise, Luther here invites us to consider the stewardship of play in this place. The text betrays an excess that our imaginations might not first imagine. Luther's exegesis is not a product that can be depleted by sharing. No, it is rather the case that in sharing it, a gain is accrued to Luther. The theme of stewardship is not so very far from his mind here. The upside-down logic of the Reign of God orders Luther's imagination. We only live by dying. We only receive by giving. Hard-earned exegesis is squandered when it is kept to the self. Space is given by God for play so that we are refreshed to the end that the products of our play are shared by those who will receive them for their flourishing in the Reign of God.

In sum, the stewardship of surplus that Luther alludes to in his exegetical comments becomes a broader trope for understanding not only the game of play but also the game of food. The logic of loaves and fishes becomes the means by which we understand why God gives us both time and space to play, to hunt, to work, to relax. What we "capture" is only received in its being given away by being shared in human community. There is an old Jewish proverb that suggests that "where there is too much, something is missing." What is missing is the gift of giving. God is the first exemplar of the gain of giving. God gives us place for play, for work, for worship, but not to the end that God is exhausted in the giving. There is no lack in God because of the gifts that God gives in giving the divine self as well as the gifts of creation. Of course, we are not God, yet that does not mean the logic of divine stewardship of giving is lost on us. No, it is rather the case that its interest is compounded. Instead of not losing in giving (as is the case with God), giving for us is itself a gift and we not only do not lose by giving, but we also accrue a gain. Yet what has this to do with place?

The above invites us to imagine that we only ever receive a place by sharing it with others. In short, hospitality of space is not so much an expectation (although it is that in a certain sense), as it is the only means by which we receive the place and its accompanying goods that are ours.[19] Sharing place was the modus operandi of the First Nations of the Americas. Theirs was an example par excellence, and the European reception of this gift was nothing short of the utter betrayal of the divine vision. In the stead of sharing what had been shared, place was hoarded as land was greedily accumulated by and for the purposes of expansion. Indigenous hospitality was not answered in kind, but with hostility. This is the sad story that place tells in our context. Yet the good news is that the land is as resilient as its first inhabitants; and as surely as the First Nations of the Americas will reclaim their place on this continent and in our histories together, the land will proclaim to us the logic of a stewardship of place that invites us into community as the first and last of the divine gifts.

KAIROTIC AND POETIC PLACE

The above ruminations on place, as illumined by poetic and metaphoric vantage points, illustrate that a certain potency attends attention to place. Place, in light of the gospel, bears the mark of cross, which points us to the God of Jesus Christ, yet in an indirect mode. It is not simply the case that in the cross I know God, but rather that at the cross, God makes the divine self known obliquely, or perhaps, indirectly. This reference to an indirect, that is, poetic, revelation speaks to Løgstrop's understanding of poetic discourse as noted above. An indirect mode of discourse makes space for an apprehension of the self to appear and with the self its primary partners in the mystery of life: God and the cosmos. In what follows I simply underscore these two modes of relationality that take place at the cross and in so doing hope to synthesize some of the preceding understandings of what it means to take place seriously, and so to imagine a kairotic place.

The noun *kairos* points to a kind of time that stands in contradiction to *chronos*. *Kairotic* time is time of insight, a time in which God breaks through to us. In what follows I underscore that we can apply, in an analogous fashion, this theme to place. To take place seriously, then, is to imagine that Paul's image of the earth giving birth to the hope that is in us—midwifed by the Spirit—cannot be construed apart from death. And so a kairotic place is a place wherein we are opened, in this instance or that, to death as both a gift and task. As noted above, the Ojibway elder Basil Johnston speaks of a First Nation understanding of the potency of place in that "certain precipices, recesses in woods, ravines, waterfalls, caves, or valleys were infused with a greater presence of Kitchi-Manitou than were others."[20]

Some places are more potent than others. Christians, too, can affirm this where the cross appears to us as a cipher for resurrection and new life. Here, and there, we see the motif of the cross in our interactions with Mother Earth. As the earth labors, we discover, in particular places, at particular times ourselves to be in a birth canal. As the earth gives birth, we see our connectivity to her in a new light. No longer do we live on the earth, but now we live with the earth. And, paradoxically, this new life is one in which we not only discover our new agency in Christ, but the agency of the earth itself. It is truly the case that in Christ, creation itself is new (2 Cor. 5:17). Certain places become for us revelations of that eternal event wherein our relationship to the earth is reframed and reformed by the Spirit's work. Kairotic places alert us to the beauty of the earth, but they do so precisely by giving us distance, or a space, from which to see the earth anew. These experiences are precisely the conditions for the possibility of exercising stewardship of creation. Yet stewardship here is radically qualified. We care for the earth as for a Mother, which precludes managing her as a resource. Rather, we honor the earth as our partner in the noble vocation of giving glory to God, and we know that serving the Lord with all of our heart, strength, and wisdom is of a piece with loving our neighbor as ourselves. Kairotic places remind us that the earth, too, is our neighbor. These cross-sections in life, those places where it becomes clear that we are dependent on the earth as our source of life, become places where we reimagine our way into the world with the task of tending the wounded Christ by caring for the earth's trauma. This is not to imagine the earth as the body of God, but to experience the earth as the locus for God's indirect, and so poetic, appearance. We turn now to imagine how a kairotic place reframes our relationship with God.

If a kairotic place is a place that allows us to renew our relationship to earth as to a Mother, how does it reframe and renew our relationship with God? In the last two sections of the above treatments of poetic ruminations, it was noted that re-creation does not preclude mourning what has passed away, and the suggestion that space, in a fashion, is non-competitive. How does the cross, as a kairotic place, advance these two notions?

At the cross, in John's gospel, Jesus "gives up the ghost" (John 19:30 KJV). He literally hands over the Spirit in the Greek text *paredōken to pneuma*. In John's gospel, events are not construed in a linear fashion, and so the giving of the Spirit occurs in a repletive fashion. The Spirit is always being given over, but at the cross—at the moment of Jesus' dying, this giving over is especially acute. With the giving of the Spirit, Jesus on the cross is differently appropriated. The passing over of Jesus from life to death enacts our reception of the Spirit to the end that from now on we will see Jesus differently: indirectly. Our hearts "burn within us" (Luke 24:32) after the fact of his revelation. And at that moment, a kind of bitter-sweet experience reframes that passing away of what was before. The new creation, then, is not a moment wherein the Spirit denies what was before, but the Spirit allows us to mourn its loss precisely so that we can receive what was before anew—and so as gifted to us by God. It is manifestly not the case that when everything passes away it ceases to be, because when it passes away it begins to be in God and so anew. Our transition into the new life, then, occurs in discrete loci wherein we see the cosmos in God. It is rather as if the cross—as it appears here and there in the manner of Johnston's description above—allows us to see the earth anew and to experience its experience of us in the guise of the parent: glad to see her children growing up, yet simultaneously wistful and rejoicing. Kairotic spaces allow us to experience the earth as Mother, and so to begin to see how we are seen: beloved. But how can we relate this to the theme of place as non-competitive, as noted in the previous chapter?

Competition seems to be definitive of being human. My promotion comes at the expense of someone being passed over. In terms of economics, a dollar accrued by me is lost by you. The logic of supply and demand is predicated on a vision of a world that is finite, and so allows the possibility, if not the necessity, of competition. Yet, is this the only way to imagine the world? Here again, the image of a kairotic place reframes first our image of God, and then our image of the world. In so doing, Christians may find that theirs is a particular way to imagine the sacred nature of space.

On the one hand, with religions the world over, we understand certain places to be sacred, or holy. On the other hand, Christianity has not inordinately privileged such places, making of pilgrimage a *sine qua non* of devotion, not salvation. Insofar as certain places have potency in a kairotic fashion, many of us will have the experience of having something of a revelatory moment at some site. Yet, we also may find that in returning to that spot, on another occasion, it fails to be sacred—at least in the same way. It now becomes sacred in the mode of memorial. I have a memory of this place as holy, and carry it with me. Its sacred potential lay in its portability. I can take this place with me. In this sense, this place has become non-competitive. Others, too, can do this. This idea is really rather analogous to the notion that God loves each of us unconditionally. Our experience of deep, abiding love is usually within the framework of a relationship that is exclusive, or at least restricted: our parents, our spouse, a special kind of friendship. Kairotic places are not restrictive, or competitive, in this fashion. An illustration might be in order.

A few years ago I went on a pilgrimage with some friends on the St. Olaf's Way in Norway. The time and place were ripe with kairotic encounters. I imagined my paternal ancestors plodding along parts of the land hosting this trail. I thought of them leaving this beautiful country in times of great trouble. I have many rich memories from that trip, yet I can be fairly certain that a return trip would be utterly different. This I know from other experiences of returning to a place that was spiritually rich, or even rich in some other sense. It is experienced differently the second time around, in part because on a return trip I would encounter something of the self that was there before. Consequently, I do not only learn something about myself on the way, but I leave something of myself behind when I pass through a place, and so I felt that I was never alone in this pilgrimage. I was mindful along the way that just as other pilgrims took something of St. Olaf's way with them when they left, they also left something of themselves behind. Kairotic places remind us of that. These are non-competitive places. In fact, when we leave something of ourselves behind, we do not accrue a loss, but a gain, and we can be sure the earth experiences the same in turn. Of course, we know that precisely because it is a divine truth first. God's giving of the divine self in creation, in redemption, and in sanctification does not deplete God because God's giving reflects the divine excess that multiplies in *koinonia*, in community.

CONCLUSION

In this chapter I have pondered the poetic potency of place, mindful that the poetry functions by means of an indirect discourse in achieving its end of creation (from *poie-ō*, Greek for I make). This creative task is facilitated by imaginative discovery, and so comparative theology as the methodology of this present work is a fit partner for the task of exploring the kairotic character of place poetically. Comparative theology is necessarily imaginative since comparison itself is "an active, at times even a playful, enterprise of deconstruction and reconstitution which, kaleidoscope-like, gives the scholar a shifting set of characteristics."[21] Engaging Indigenous traditions imaginatively in this exercise has been fruitful in causing us to consider the earth as the source of diversity, and so a kind of pedagogue in the gift of diversity, a point of departure for the exercise of comparative theology. Indigenous traditions are but one way by which Christian theology can have its certainty unsettled. The gain of this uncertainty, as was noted above, is a capacity to see the world in a new modality: one in which ambiguity is generative and Christians are pushed to our edges, where we meet our neighbors with the conviction that kairotic space is non-competitive. There is no market to corner in meeting the divine. The divine is met in cooperation, not competition, and so we are driven to our edges where we encounter the other in those in-between spaces where both we and they step outside of our comfort zones as we pursue together the truth that drives us outside of ourselves.

> In this respect, the challenge of comparative theology, itself an offspring of some cultural and religious interstices of our time, is then precisely to seek out further, or to create, if necessary, these in-between spaces. . . . because comparative theology is a theological discipline, the in-between spaces here should also be understood, ultimately, as a milieu of divine revelation, a space of our struggle to understand God better.[22]

In the final chapter, then, we allow this poetic imagination to guide us as we step into this kairotic, third space where I propose that the between of two faiths is a locus of hope.

NOTES

1. Heid E. Erdrich, "The Theft Outright," Poetry Foundation, accessed March 28, 2020, https://www.poetryfoundation.org/poems/89050/the-theft-outright.
2. From Seamus Heaney, "Triptych: Sibyl," in *Field Work: Poems* (New York: Farrar, 1976), 5.

3. LW 31, 344.
4. See Johnston, *The Manitous*, 116.
5. Suicide (assisted or not) is not even an exception that proves the rule because even this dying is nothing but a summation of a thousand deaths that have led to this death.
6. Anne Michaels, *Fugitive Pieces* (Toronto: McClelland and Stewart Inc., 1996), 53.
7. Johnston, *Ojibway Heritage*, 49, 50.
8. As noted in chapter 1 earlier, note 33.
9. See Simone Pétrement, *Simone Weil: A Life*, trans. Raymond Rosenthal (New York: Pantheon Books, 1976), 462. The book references a letter from Weil to Joë Bousquet, dated April 13, 1942.
10. Contra clear evidence to the contrary in Rom. 8:21.
11. Tomas Tranströmer, Excerpt from "Out in the Open" from *The Deleted World: Poems*, versions by Robin Robertson (Toronto: Anansi Press, 2011), 21.
12. See Westhelle, *Eschatology and Space* and Jorgenson "Empire, Eschatology and Stolen Land," 115–122.
13. These *"solae"* (instances of "alone") are most commonly iterated as "Christ alone, grace alone and faith alone." To these might be added scripture, or the cross. In the Reformed tradition *soli Deo Gloria* (to God alone the glory) is a traditional fifth to the fourth of scripture.
14. See Johnston, *Ojibway Heritage*, 149–171 for some instances of such characters in the Ojibway tradition.
15. It is interesting to note that Schleiermacher, in a sermon on the passion and resurrection of Christ, was at pains to demonstrate the connection between the crucified and resurrected Christ since this event is an analogue of our redemption. For this reason, he can write "When the old Adam or Eve of sin has died, and we now live in Christ and with him in God, then we are indeed the same people who were before." See Friedrich Schleiermacher, *Sämmtliche Werke II*, 2 (Berlin: G. Reimer, 1821), 180. The translation is my own of *Wenn der alte Mensch der Sünde gestorben ist, und wir nun in Christo und mit ihm Gott leben, so sind wir doch dieselben, die wir vorher gewesen sind*.
16. LW 14, 110.
17. Miikka E. Anttila, "Music," in *Engaging Luther*, 215.
18. Ibid.
19. See Laksana, "Comparative Theology," 18, wherein he identifies that the task of pilgrimage schools us in hospitality, a point of signal importance for Comparative Theology.
20. Johnston, *The Manitous*, 6.
21. Jonathan Z. Smith, *Divine Drudgery: On the Comparison of Early Christianities and the Religions of Late Antiquity* (Chicago: University of Chicago Press, 1990), 53.
22. Laksana, "Comparative Theology," 7.

Chapter 5

Place at the Margins, Hope, and Living Interfaithfully

LEARNING ON THE LAND

A theology of place is contextually attentive, and so theologians of place are eager to learn from those who know their *loci* intimately. On Turtle Islands, the First Peoples call us to

Recognize whose lands these are on which we stand.
Ask the deer, turtle, and the crane.
Make sure the spirits of these lands are respected and treated with goodwill.[1]

The land has a story that demands a hearing. When we are attentive to this, we sometimes discover that certain places are kairotic, and as such may well be described as sacred. Thus, Protestant Christians who are inclined to accept such a notion might be inclined to affirm that what makes a site sacred is not *something*, but the divine fiat that it should be so, which may or may not be enduring in such a place. Sites that are received as sacred for Christians are signed with the cross and so remind us that re-creation is not the obliteration of creation, but its re-construal to the end that we experience the earth as a Mother who births us into a new kind of agency by the grace of Word and Spirit. This agency is not described with the logic of a zero-sum game. We do not give up ourselves by giving away ourselves, but like the earth, we finally come to be most fully in giving away who we are in serving love. Certain places under the aegis of the Spirit make this plain. These places I have called kairotic. They enable us to take all place seriously and all space as sacred, and so foster in us an attitude of expectation, as was evident in my example of such a place in St. Olaf's Way, a pilgrimage I made in the land of my ancestors some years ago.

The following year, I made another spiritual journey. This time it was (a bit) closer to home. The Cypress Hills are some 3,000 km northwest from where I now live and 500 km southeast from where I grew up. This is a place of profound historic importance in Western Canada, a land of some spiritual intensity for First Nations on the Plains and of historic importance in that the first fort (Fort Walsh) of the Northwest Mounted Police (later to become known as the Royal Canadian Mounted Police/Gendarmerie royale du Canada) was on its eastern edge.[2] The establishment of this fort was purported to be an intervention by the Tory government of the day as a way to keep wolfers and rum runners at bay. The former were those who used poisoned buffalo meat to expedite their search for wolf carcasses to be sold to fur traders. The latter were those who used rum sales to Indigenous people to expedite their search for easier riches.[3] While keeping these folk and their mischiefs at bay was, indeed, one role of the NWMP on the newly claimed territories, it was also true that the John A. McDonald government of the day intended to use the presence of the NWMP to encourage Indigenous groups to sign treaties and so to clear the plains for the project of a building a railroad for the cementing of a national identity.[4] My colleague and friend Matthew Anderson, a specialist in pilgrimage studies, had proposed walking the NWMP patrol trail (some 300 km from Wood Mountain to Cypress Hills) in solidarity with Indigenous people who suffer still from the legacy of colonialism. This trail, of long-standing significance to the Assiniboine, Cree, Gros Ventres, Blackfoot, and Métis became the path along which NWMP traversed in this task of keeping the aforementioned wolfers and rum runners at bay and in keeping the peace with the Lakota, traveling north after the Battle of the Little Bighorn in 1876.[5]

As noted above, the path to Cypress Hills was significant to Indigenous peoples because these hills were thought to be spiritually potent, a land of spiritual quests.[6] Moreover, the Hills themselves are a beautiful aberration on the hauntingly intoxicating Great Plains, which was once the basin of an ancient inland sea. The Cypress Hills are, in words of Savage, "a course jumble of stones that had washed out of the young Rocky Mountains and had been carried eastward and northeastward by great, gnashing rivers during the Miocene era."[7] They tower on the great prairie landscape, with folds of terrain bending down in valleys of hundreds of feet prior to the ascent of the Hills proper. The flora and fauna of the region are more akin to that of the Rocky Mountains some 500 km to the west. Ray Aldred notes that the Cypress Hills "were and are sacred to the tribal groups of the northern plains. As such, this area was considered international territory."[8] These lands were preferred by Indigenous communities as sites for reserves, but they were forcibly removed from the hills and environs upon the decision to build the national railway through southern Saskatchewan.[9]

Anderson saw this trail as an especially fitting location for a sojourn of reconciliation. Various people—including those from First Nations in the area—joined him for stretches along the way. My wife and I joined him and others for the last 100 km. At about day six we came upon an especially interesting site where flat prairie gave way to a series of deep valleys pleating into one another with a slowly trickling creek meandering below. As we looked around us, we could see dozens of groups of stones set in circles. These were tipi rings, and they marked places where groups of First Nations had set up tipis in their journeys across the prairie.[10] The sheer number in this particular convergence of valleys suggested that it was something of a meeting point. Many of us went off on our own for a bit, sitting in the midst or at the edge of these rings, sculpted by stones that might have been either hundreds or thousands of years old. There was a palpable sense of a profound presence there, and I reached into my pocket and pulled out a bit of tobacco, and laid it at one of these stones, feeling the need to honor that moment and most especially that place.[11]

We all later spoke of the power of that particular place. In a way, we all felt touched by the sense that we were not alone there, and the circles that sketched a center spoke to us of the truth that paying attention to edges is a spiritual mandate (Matt. 25:31–46). As noted in the previous chapters, edges are potent places, a lesson we learned deeply in our souls out on this prairie landscape, miles from "civilization." Here we learned anew that knowing the whole demands moving to the edge, the contours of our existence. The edges, or the boundaries, of our experience are where we encounter the other, and most importantly, where we encounter the One in whom "we live and move and have our being" (Acts 17:28) who wills our walking outside of our comfort zones for the sake of our Mother the earth, others, and ourselves. In a way, the edge of our existence is where we most experience hope. I might venture that hope is located at the edge or limit of our experiences, at those places where we stretch toward the future that bids us die so that we might live. In what follows, I want to explore this theme as I engage the possibility of taking place seriously at the margins, where we discover that the other is not altogether foreign, but also interior, and so urgently in need of discovery so that we might better know who we are and the One who made us so.

In what follows, then, I will locate hope as especially potent at the margins, and point to it as a bridge that links various modes of being in the world. I will next attend to the observation that at the edge of our collective lives, religion rubs shoulder with religion. And so, hope invites us to think about the interfaced character of living our faiths. This interface admits a kind of permeability and yet a sort of boundary. This will lead me to consider a recent document by the World Council of Churches as a resource for thinking about a theology of religions in light of some of what I have learned from the First

Nations of Turtle Island. In so doing, I am going to commend the need to live interfaithfully, a word I use to describe this necessary interface of faithful living. First, then, to hope.

HOPE AND HUMAN EXPERIENCE

Home's the place we head for in our sleep.
Boxcars stumbling north in dreams
don't wait for us. We catch them on the run.[12]

Hope, Fear and Humiliation: A Secular Exploration of Hope

One pathway into the mystery of hope is *via negativa*, wherein we ponder what it is not. Perhaps nothing is so antipathetic to hope as colonization, which runs counter to the current of hope in that its goal is totalizing and its standard is certainty. Catherine Keller notes that "[c]ertainty allows the conquest of other, which it simplifies as an object."[13] Perhaps no people know this reality as intimately as the Indigenous people objectified for the sake of the *modus operandi* of efficiency in the exploits of the empire. Hope, of course, runs counter-current to this certainty that funds efficiency, and so invites us to think of its role in a world bending under the weight of colonialism in its geopolitical guises.

Dominique Moïsi explores the theme of hope in *The Geopolitics of Emotion: How Cultures of Fear, Humiliation and Hope are Re-shaping the World*.[14] In this provocative book he suggests that an economic or social accounting of the effects of globalization is not yet enough. He proposes to make some sense of geopolitics by way of analysis of the emotions, principally the emotions of fear, hope, and humiliation. As he works his way through these, he proposes that each of these three emotions is a primary driver for different cultures.[15] Although his analytic is not driven by questions of place, these geopolitical interest of his study presupposes topological points of intersection: place matters when pondering emotions since many emotions are born in particular locales. This is as true for the body politic as it is for the individual body.

Moïsi suggests that the arrival of global problems such as climate change, terrorism, health epidemics, and internal conflicts has become the cause of global insecurity.[16] At a global level, such insecurity continually raises questions of identity: people groups are forced to think through who they are at a global level. We all, in fact, are geopolitical actors because even if we refuse to engage the world, the world engages us with these and other problems. The world cannot be kept at bay. Borders are porous, no matter how high we build fences, no matter how thick our walls are, and in the face of the world we need to take a stand, take a place; we need to find our space in the world. Global troubles press upon us and impress on us the need to identify ourselves.[17] As cultures we are called to answer the question: Who are we? This inescapable question comes to us as a crisis, and as many of us may recall, the Chinese character for crisis also signals opportunity. And so, we respond to this crisis in various ways. According to Moïsi, the response to the question "Who are we?" points to confidence or its lack among people groups. Here he introduces the three abovementioned emotions of fear, humiliation, and hope as expressions of our confidence or insecurity. These three are natural emotions and expected public responses to challenges insofar as they also have a communal character.[18] In a fashion, confidence is a kind of master description that links fear, humiliation, and love together. Although humiliation and fear are typically viewed as negative, Moïsi claims all three play an important part in defining who I am as a person and who we are as people. Hope is a fuel for life, fear is necessary for survival, and humiliation in small doses stimulates hard work.[19] And so, to give an example, if I were to give a public lecture on the topic of this chapter, my hope would be that the talk would inspire interfaith conversations and relations; my fear would be that if I fail in my task I could inspire either rigid dogmatism or mindless relativism, and so in order to avoid the humiliation that would demonstrate my gross incompetence, I would work hard to pull such a presentation together in a cogent, convincing, and winsome manner. Moïsi helps us to attend to hope as both personal and communal. But what does he understand hope to be? We read:

> Hope is confidence. In the Western world the notion of hope has two different connotations. There is hope in the spiritual sense of the term, the belief in the salvation of humanity through the redemption from sin. But there is also the secular meaning of the term. Hope is trust in one's identity, in one's ability to interact positively in the world. ... Hope is the opposite of resignation, a form of trust that pushes us to move toward others, to accept without fear how they differ from us.[20]

Hope is many things: confidence, belief, trust, the opposite of resignation, acceptance. These all seem helpful and what goes without saying needs to be said: hope is an emotion with a universal reach. To be without hope is to begin to cease to be. We need hope to live. Indigenous scholar Neal McLeod writes that "[o]ur stories give us voice, hope, and a place in the world."[21]

McLeod underscores the power of narrative to generate hope, but he also notes how this hope is related to having voice and place. These latter two are especially pertinent in the context of the history of colonialism in the Americas. Official policies of governments have included the attempt to eradicate Indigenous languages, and so their voice in service of making them "fit citizens" in service of the empire. In so doing, the intent of the government was that Indigenous peoples would leave land reserved for them, and thereby "clear the plains" as noted above. With the erasure of voice and place, hope evaporates. McLeod proposes the power of a "Cree narrative memory" in order to secure voice, hope, and place. He notes:

> Cree narratives are held within oral traditions and social relationships and provide a counterpoint to the narratives of non-Cree society. The activity and process of these narratives challenge the hegemony of the mainstream discourse, which has often been conflated with notions of "progress" that have ultimately undermined Cree narrative memory and been used as a tool of conquest.[22]

Colonial powers strove to displace Indigenous people and eradicate their language in order to deprive them of hope, knowing that hope is the air we breathe, the water we drink, and the gravity that keeps us grounded. Hope is the currency of life. McLeod demonstrates that a Cree narrative memory is a refusal to bow to colonial machinations. Indigenous peoples across Turtle Island know well that the stories we tell ourselves shape our way of being. But for those of us who are not Indigenous, what stories might inform us in service of granting us hope that sustains, a voice that speaks truth to power, and a healthy and holy relationship to place? I turn to that task now.

Hope as Abandonment: A Theology of Hope

I am a Christian, and so my reflections on hope emerge from that confession. In what follows I will make some very brief comments on the character of hope as expressed by an important Jesuit theologian of the 20th century, Karl Rahner. I will then engage a few other thinkers to fill out something of a rudimentary Christian theology of hope before moving the conversation to the theme of the margins, where what I have said will become clearly highlighted in its illumination by our neighbors; the religions in their varied expressions.

In an article titled "A Theology of Hope" Rahner provides us with a few points of entrée for a discussion of hope.[23] In sum, we find that at the heart of his understanding of hope is the assertion that hope is abandonment to God.[24] Hope is finally an outward turn from human self-obsession to divine expectation. Hope happens as the human is re-oriented, as the human turns to the east, where the sun rises and newness dawns. By letting go of self-obsession, by refusing to see "me" as a project to be mastered, and by turning to God as the source of grace, ability, and passion for the well-being in the world, the faithful become hopeful. Rahner did not restrict this hope to the Christian but considered all people who follow their conscience to its source to be people of such hope.[25] Moreover, even people who are not people of faith experience hope, albeit as a profane hope, in his view. This profane hope is described as a provisional hope that disappears once what has been hoped for arrives.[26] Of course, all of us know of this hope: the hope that one day our mortgage will be paid off; the hope that we will find a meaningful job that meets our needs, etc. This profane, or perhaps we might call it provisional, hope points us to an enduring hope, a sacred hope. Here Rahner refers to the famous statement by the Apostle Paul in 1 Corinthians 13:13 where he writes: "And now faith, hope, and love abide, these three; and the greatest of these is love." These three abide. Unlike profane hope, sacred hope abides; it endures into eternity. Of course, this assertion makes no sense for a profane understanding of hope, wherein hope disappears once what is hoped for arrives. But Rahner defines hope by beginning with the bible's assertion that hope endures into eternity. This is the beginning point for a theological understanding of hope, and for this reason, Rahner understands hope to be that outward from self-abandonment to God.[27] Hope is intimately related to faith and love, and these three, according to Aquinas are theological virtues.[28] Faith, hope, and love, according to this 13th-century theological giant, are first understood to be what God does for us as God establishes each of them in us. Rahner learned from Aquinas that hope is first something that God does to us. Hope is God robbing us of self-confidence and grounding our confidence in God; turning us toward God. Hope is God reminding us that we have a reason to hope, and we are not that reason. Pam McCarroll writes that the shape of hope is waiting and this waiting takes place at the foot of the cross.[29] Luther spoke persuasively, in the Christian perspective, of the cross as that place where God works unexpectedly by means of suffering such that we know that God's modus operandi is to use our weakness to point to divine strength, our confusion to point to divine wisdom, and our incapacity to point to God's capabilities.[30] But *where* does this all happen? What is the place of hope—both in the sense of location and purpose—in our lives?

Luther invited us to turn our attention away from centers of power to see hope. Hope does not happen where power rests on its laurels. If we want to glimpse hope, Wall Street and other centers of power will not be where we need to go, but to edges, limits, and margins. We turn now to the margins.

Hope at the Margins

Some years ago, my wife, my youngest daughter, and I visited India. We were invited to the wedding of a family member of some Indo-Canadian friends. The wedding was to take place in Mumbai. Upon our return, people often asked us about our experience. Sometimes I led by saying that it was altogether too short, which was true. Sometimes I began by saying it was colorful, which was also true. But above all else, I would describe our experience as one in which we found the country incredibly hospitable.

At an airport, while standing beside my seated wife, a gentleman insisted I take his seat. When I hesitated, he insisted, saying, "Please, you are our guest." This stranger considered me his guest. At another airport, another gentleman insisted on sending his sandwich with me on the plane since there would be no meal on our domestic flight. Everywhere we went we were received graciously. We told our tour driver of this, and he—a Christian—reminded us of the Sanskrit phrase:

Atithi Devo Bhava
The guest manifests God.[31]

The Indians we met were very hospitable. Of course, we did not have to go to India to encounter hospitality. Despite colonial designs, the First Peoples of the Americas have demonstrated a hospitality that is instructive for all on Turtle Island. Randy Woodley notes that "[h]ospitality and generosity are the natural economy in Indigenous community."[32] Further,

> the problem of America the nation-state is not its immigrants but white supremacy and the corresponding values that prop up hostile and egregious policies that keep others out. From an Indigenous American perspective, these policies of unwelcome defy millennia-old values of hospitality; they erode the sovereignty of Indigenous peoples; and they perpetuate a historic bias toward white supremacy.[33]

The narrative of the land is one of welcome, but this is a narrative that has been undone by colonial design. Jacques Derrida spoke at length of hospitality as something that undoes our mania for having everything under control.[34] Empire is decidedly about having everything under control, and so is hostile to hospitality, which takes one to the edge, the margin, and the perimeter in openness, generosity, and gratitude.

Hospitality, above all else, occurs first at the door, at the entrance to the house, compound, tent, or airport. Hospitality occurs at points of entry, where the stranger is encountered, and the subject is face to face with the unknown person, with a face that is not a face in the mirror. Paradoxically, it is precisely in our treatment of the other that a mirror arrives. We begin to know who we are as we examine how we treat the sojourner or wayfarer. Edges are revelatory and so can be places where changes take place. The edge is where we grow, and so it is aptly called a growing edge. Of course, we grow and change at our center, our core, our *coeur*, our heart—but the edge demands special attention.

Religious edges are the places where the religions encounter the world, and in encountering the world religions encounter one another. It is the place where religions have that curious, and sometimes difficult but often heady experience of being host, and of being guest. Derrida writes at length about the difficulty of this being both guest and host.[35] Grace is needed at the door, port, and even airport, where we import and export our expectations, our protestations, and, above all, our surprise.

At the periphery, or the edge, of our existence we experience again and again that we are cast upon resources beyond our own. We are cast upon God who surprises us. It seems that it is at the margins that we are forced to hope. So many things are beyond our control at the edges of our existence. The guest comes to the host unbidden, and the host does not get to choose his or her guest.

Being a guest or a host is often out of our control even while our mode of being such is *the* ethical task of our life. Moreover, we often find that the boundary between being guest and host is sometimes itself permeable. This might be especially evident for settlers in North America, where we who were received by the Indigenous now receive immigrants.[36] These immigrants whom we now host—sometimes willing, sometimes not—increasingly can be identified as religious others. Further, the Indigenous people of this land have also been religious others to Christians in their traditional spiritualities, as well as in their—to many Christians' consternation—capacity to engage both traditional and Christian ways of being. They show us something about living at religious boundaries. We turn now to the task of living faithfully in an interfaith era; we turn to the task of living interfaithfully.

LIVING INTERFAITHFULLY

I will share these stories
but I will not share
those from which I will never crawl.[37]

Facing Reality: Living Inter-

Our storied character in North America is both beautiful and painful, rooted in our experiences and our reflections on these in conversation with our deepest held convictions about God, the world, and the self. Some of these can be told, and some inform us of a peculiar intensity beyond the tellings. But one thing that is certain about these is that they are plural. Religious pluralism is a fact in much of North America.

In my context, one could go to Statistics Canada to point to the burgeoning reality of religious plurality in Canada, or one could go for a drive and find Mosques in Northern Alberta's logging towns, Sikh Gurdwaras across the road from Ontario cornfields, and Hindu Temples spread across suburbia from coast to coast. These religious homes are reminders that immigrants bring with them what they most need and, for many, that need includes stories, rituals, and commandments that have ultimate or transcendent origin in their estimation. The days are gone when religions stayed within borders, although we know from the history of our First Peoples that those days never really existed.

Susan Neylan, in a work problematizing the too-common assumption that Indigenous peoples on the west coast of the land some call Canada were coerced into abandoning their spiritualities and worldviews in order to become Christians, argues that

> despite missionary agendas and objectives, conversion to Christianity did not constitute a replacement of pre-existing spiritual beliefs. Rather, pre-existing Aboriginal and Christian frameworks of understanding power complemented as much as they clashed with one another. Missions, thus, were sites of contested meanings that reveal the hegemony of colonization, and Native roles in missionization are central to perceiving this very process.[38]

Neylan notes that the image of the hapless Native forced into conversion without agency simply does not hold true in her analysis of the Tsimshian encounters with Christianity in the 19th century. She notes how the practice of augmenting Tsimshian spiritual life with external forms existed prior to contact. So, even while Christian missions all too often were "intrusive, coercive, and destructive," its adoption was not without the agency of the Tsimshian in a modality that did not result in the obliteration of Indigenous spiritualities and worldviews.[39] She notes strategies of syncretism, convergence, and dualism at work in the interrelationship of these two spiritual worldviews.[40] In a study of a contemporary situation on the Atlantic coast, Sarah J. King notes how the Mi'kmaw people were able to integrate and draw upon traditional Mi'kmaw, traditional Christianity, and Charismatic Christianity simultaneously as resources in trials they faced in the Burnt Church crisis.[41] To give another example, Tink Tinker marvelously relates a tale in which Indigenous people harvesting a Christmas tree involves "a thorough mixture of Christian prayers and traditional Indian tribal prayers."[42]

In sum, the First Peoples of Turtle Island have been living with religious pluralism for a very long time. Non-indigenous Christians are slowly beginning to work through what this might mean for them and would be well served by attending to their voices and their experiences. Of course, there has also been important Christian work regarding religious pluralism. We begin with the latter and turn to the former at the end of the chapter.

In 2005 the World Council of Churches made available an unofficial document titled "Religious Plurality and Christian Self Understanding."[43] This document was a timely and significant theological endeavor, penned by twenty scholars representing different constituencies in the life of the WCC. Although it does not represent the views of the WCC, the document provides the reader with a measured sense of some of the ways in which religious pluralism is construed in the Christian tradition. Moreover, it articulates ways in which former statements by the WCC are in need of further clarification. Above all, the document invites the reader to ponder the possibility of a theology of religions. This, in itself, is a bold and important advance: an attempt to speak about the religions in relation to divine action and not merely as failed human attempts at appropriating the divine. The most recent statements by the WCC had noted that Christianity, while affirming religious plurality as a good, needed to be held in tension with the affirmation that Jesus alone is the way to salvation. As of late, it was felt that more needed to be said.

As we read the document, it is interesting to note that, in good Trinitarian fashion, the reader is invited to think about creation, salvation, and the work of the Spirit. Creation is an important starting point and, building on early documents, it is affirmed that God is present in the plurality of the religions.[44] This confession that God is present in the religions is then related to Jesus's *modus operandi*: a posture of openness and a way of welcome. Just as Jesus concretized radical openness in unconditional love Christians, according to the document, are called to balance fidelity to Christ and openness to the religious other.[45] The document defines hospitality "primarily as a radical openness to others based on the dignity of all."[46] The dignity of all is not, then, what God creates by saving us but instead the reason God saves us. God creates the world, the human, and the universe as good and for this reason all have dignity. This dignity presumes plurality. We might want to say that the dignity of all is written into the poetics of creation and is, in fact, expressed in diversity. Monocultures are, in fact, not sustainable in the long run, and there might be room for Christian theologians to reflect on the transferability of this truth about creation to the phenomenon of religious diversity. Religious plurality, in this perspective, is not a problem, but a possibility. Moreover, the document helpfully proposes that this religious diversity has spiritual utility insofar as our learning from other religious traditions enables us "to understand anew the deposit of faith already given us."[47] This is, of course, an astounding acknowledgment: that Christians after visiting the foreign "lands" of other religions can return to their own with fresh appreciation for "home." Yet we might want to ask if something other than that already given to us is received in this encounter. Could it be that we learn something new from other religions? This is an open question and it presses upon our concern to be faithful to the faith that first claimed us. We turn now to that theme.

Facing our Roots: Living Faithfully

Perhaps one of the pieces of the WCC document that I most like is its honest appraisal of religions. On the one hand, it sees all of them—Christianity included—as signs of God at work. On the other hand, it is not naïve. The document helpfully warns against the dangers of a "romantic attitude" toward religions.[48] The caution is due to the history of religions' complicity in the empire. Religions have served as the engine for the vehicles of conquest and crusade and have been complicit in empire building. And yet there is hope resident in an understanding of religions as "spiritual journeys."

Religions in such an imaginary are rather like nomads: religions are on the move, sometimes traveling with one another and sometimes sojourning on their own. In my estimation, living faithfully—as one component of interfaithful living—is accepting our identity as nomads and recognizing that we live on the way, in a journey wherein we wager our life of faith. Such journeys presume transformation in service of human flourishing and of renewal of the cosmos as the sine qua non of authentic religious existence.[49] It seems helpful to me that this marker of religious identity in *service* is so prominent in the document. If religion is not a resource for the healing of creation and peace among people, it has drastically lost its way. Beyond this fundamental social dimension of religions, the document also helpfully addresses the manner in which pastoral questions attend our apprehension of the religions and underlines four ways in which religious plurality is engaged by the faithful.[50] It is noted that some people use resources from other religious traditions "to deepen" their Christian life; some experience other religious traditions as a home away from home to the end that they experience "double belonging"; some engage multifaith realities in the home as a result of marriage, and in the public in the practice of multifaith prayer and peace-making; and still others in interfaith agitation for justice and peace.[51] As noted above, Indigenous peoples have been able to creatively integrate their spiritualities and worldviews with Christianity for some time. Religions are differently engaged by the faithful, but in a situation of plurality not engaging them is not possible.[52] So we see, then, that living faithfully does not mean living on our own.

To be faithful is to be with your neighbor and so to see your interdependence. Nowhere is this as clearly seen as in the Indigenous phrase "all my relations." Randy Woodley explains it as follows:

> The idea that all people and things are related to each other includes all of humanity. This idea opens us to the possibility of once again becoming the family we already are. By realizing the connectedness of humankind to all animal life, we become aware of new possibilities for learning and maintaining a concern for the preservation of all things.[53]

Shawn Wilson further illumines the power of relationality in asserting that in an Indigenous worldview, "reality is relationships, or sets of relationships."[54] I am, then, because of my relationship to the cosmos. Living with integrity, then, is to act with others for the well-being of the cosmos. This being-with reminds us that we live as followers of the God described as Immanuel: "God-with us." Because it is the nature of God to be with us, we who are with God seek to be with the other. But how shall we be with them? I want us to imagine a way of being with that brings together this interfaith reality and being faithful; I want us to imagine a way of being-with that is living interfaithfully and which calls us to engage the kairotic places that make this possible.

Face to Face: Living Interfaithfully

The WCC document wisely pairs the theme of journey with that of hospitality. Hospitality is, of course, a provocative means by which to ponder the phenomenon of the religions. The document rightly addresses it as both opportunity and risk.[55] The sojourner calls the householder to the vocation of a host and the host's hospitality makes a guest of the sojourner. The encounter at the door is transformative. But we might ask what we do with this encounter.

Is the other simply a curiosity to the end that interfaith experiences are a kind of tourism wherein we simply stop by and observe the other for our entertainment? This surely happens, but it need not. In fact, what I want to suggest is that thinking that we can engage other religions without being changed by them (for good or for ill) is a denial of our history. As we consider the trajectory of the history of Christianity, we realize that it not only engages other faiths when it meets them at the door—as host or as guest—but that its own faithful acts are themselves often interfaith events. This is first experienced in our reading of the Hebrew Bible. Christianity, in adopting another religion's text—albeit with its own hermeneutical sensibilities—is an instance of an interfaith engagement.[56] Beyond this, of course, interfaith engagement is also regularly experienced in our liturgical appropriation of the so-called pagan practices (one thinks of the use of the Christmas tree, the celebration of Christ's birth at the winter solstice, the celebration of All Saints Day on Samhain, etc.). While we may (rightly) understand these practices as "baptized" we also recall that baptism is not sheer erasure of created reality. In Christian thought, baptismal water is a potent trope which leverages both the drowning and the growth potential of water. Water signals both condemnation and affirmation. Our Christian ancestors, at least prior to its establishment in the Constantine era, recognized good in other religious traditions.[57] These goods remain resident within Christianity as an affirmation of what promoted human flourishing in other religious traditions. What has sometimes been called Christianity's syncretic character is not merely a strategy for continuity, but a theological judgment about the goodness of creation, including some strategic apprehensions of humanity's religious propensities. Unfortunately, Christianity under the aegis of empire in North America has paid too little attention to this imperative. But still, there are instances within Christian practice that speak clearly to this theological assessment of the goodness of creation in the broadest sense.

But I want to push this theme further as evidenced in the practice of the Lord's Supper. Christians hold a variety of views about what this practice means, and I do not want to minimize these differences since the practice of eating bread and drinking wine is not shared by all Christians. For many of the Christians, however, this sacred meal is understood to be an encounter with Jesus in some fashion, be it physically, spiritually, or commemoratively. Jesus is somehow understood to be present in this holiest of moments, even while there is contention both within and across Christian denominations about the mode of this presence. Unfortunately, this contention means that Christians too rarely ask, "Who was Jesus? Who is Jesus?" at this meal. The gospels portray him as a teacher of Israel, as a Rabbi who is a faithful Jew.[58] In a sense, then, the presence of Jesus at our most sacred meal makes it an interfaith event. When we commune, we are living interfaithfully as we gather locally to celebrate about the presence of the Lord.

This image, fittingly, brings us back to the topic at hand. This event we call the Lord's Supper takes *place kairotically*. The space marked by altar, font, and pulpit hosts the event of the presence of love at the meal. The term *presence* as applied to Jesus (in one guise or another, even if only in the mode of memorial) is instructive, as was noted above.[59] Certain places become sacred, if but for a moment, and for Christians the locus of the Eucharist—as an interfaith event—is a prime example. Kairotic places have an interfaith edge. How, then, might this relate to my experience at the tipi rings and how does my experience of Eucharist in my local church meet the experience of leaving a piece of tobacco under a rock on a hill so very far away? How was this an instance of living interfaithfully, and how did this place provide me with hope? Perhaps some comment on the activity of laying tobacco might first be appropriate.

Many First Nations consider tobacco to be one of the sacred medicines given by the Creator.[60] It is traditionally given to someone when asking them to perform a ceremony, or to provide a teaching, or to give counsel. It is also often laid down when entering a new territory or waterway.[61] These two actions are not disparate. The congruence lay in the Indigenous understanding that land has an agency that demands respect. This is critically important. Ray Aldred notes that "the land is the soul of our Cree people."[62] The place where we are demands that all that we do, including our religious doings, are to be done in a way that respects the territory in which we do it. When Christians pray, their prayers should be informed by and made for the land and the people that are supported by it. The land itself has a spirituality that is evident in the First Peoples of it, and so we know that on Turtle Island, the spirituality of the land is hospitality and generosity, and so this is demanded of Christians as they practice their faith on this land. I was mindful of this, as I laid down the tobacco that day.

At the school where I teach, we regularly give tobacco to elders, speakers, singers, etc., whom we ask to lead us in moments of learning. This is understood to be a sign of respect, and my action at the tipi rings was simply an instance of this. I felt indebted to that place for the profoundly deep experience that touched me there at the edge of the tipi ring. I might name this experience the sense of the presence of the ancestors of the peoples of that land. Their presence can be variously understood, but like most mysterious experiences, it is somehow betrayed when over-analyzed. In some ways, this mirrors the Christian experience of the Eucharist. Here, too, I meet ancestors whose presence points me to the One who is the source of faith, hope, and love for Christians.[63] This hope, in a profound way, resonated with the sense of gratitude and awe I experience on the Great Plain. Despite the many injustice Indigenous peoples across North America have suffered, they stand on the shoulders of ancestors who support them in important ways. Christians might find an analogue in the "cloud of witnesses" surrounding those who lay aside sin in walking in the way of Jesus. In both instances, a certain place pointed and points me to the hope found in our not being on our own. I looked outward: penultimately to faithful ancestors but ultimately to the One who provides hope.

CONCLUSION

In this chapter I have explored liminal places as especially kairotic. By beginning with an experience on the land, I attempted to anchor this theme in the concrete. In so doing, I discovered kairotic places at the margins to be *loci* of great hope, a theme which I explored in both secular and theological modalities. I named the experience of living at margins as living interfaithfully, using the Indigenous practice of laying down tobacco as an instantiation of an interfaith event, which led me to ponder communion as an interfaith occurrence in the Christian tradition.

On the Great Plains, I learned a lesson that I learn anew every time I take communion and in my interaction with Indigenous people practicing their traditional beliefs. God meets us at the limits of our experience to remind us that God is profoundly present in all of our lives. In both sacred circles and communion circles, I am reminded that place matters, and so should be taken seriously for what it is: a creation of God that provides the condition for the possibility of the hope that is within us (1 Pt. 3:15). This hope not only serves to sustain my faith but makes possible those encounters wherein I discover anew how many and varied are the works of God (Ps. 104:24) in creating each and every person I encounter, and those places that facilitate those encounters to the end that they reveal themselves to be holy, and so to be taken seriously.

NOTES

1. Joy Harjo, "Conflict Resolution for Holy Beings," Poetry Foundation, accessed March 30, 2020, https://www.poetryfoundation.org/poems/141847/conflict-resolution-for-holy-beings.

2. In what follows I draw upon Candace Savage, *A Geography of Blood: Unearthing Memory from a Prairie Landscape* (Toronto: Greystone Books, 2012) and James Daschuk, *Clearing the Plains: Disease, Politics of Starvation, and the Loss of Aboriginal Life* (Regina: University of Regina Press, 2013).

3. See Savage, *Geography*, 103, 104.

4. Daschuk, *Clearing*, 108–109.

5. See "Fort Walsh to Wood Mountain – North West Mounted Police Trail," Saskatchewan History and Folklore Society, accessed July 2, 2020, http://www.shfs.ca/trails.

6. "Cypress Hills," The Canadian Encyclopedia, accessed December 12, 2018, https://www.thecanadianencyclopedia.ca/en/article/cypress-hills. See Kovach, *Indigenous Methodologies*, 71–74, who discusses the theme of sacred places.

7. Savage, *Geography*, 57.

8. Ray Aldred, "A Shared Narrative," in Strangers in This World: Multireligious Reflections on Immigration, eds. Hussam S. Timani, Allen G. Jorgenson, Alexander Y. Hwang (Minneapolis: Fortress Press, 2015), 202.

9. Daschuk, *Clearing*, 123.

10. Savage, *Geography*, 81–85.

11. I provide some reflection on this action at the end of this chapter.

12. Louise Erdrich, "Indian Boarding School: The Runaways," Poetry Foundation, accessed March 27, 2020, https://www.poetryfoundation.org/poems/43079/indian-boarding-school-the-runaways.

13. Catherine Keller, *Political Theology of the Earth: Our Planetary Emergency and the Struggle for a New Republic* (New York: Columbia University Press, 2018), 15.

14. Dominique Moïsi, *The Geopolitics of Emotion: How Cultures of Fear, Humiliation and Hope are Reshaping the World* (New York: Anchor, 2010).

15. While he problematically identifies humiliation as a global phenomenon related to Islam's loss of its once glorious past (81) and the West's inability to set the global agenda with fear (90), I suspect that most would still see his interest in seeing emotions as public phenomena to be important.

16. Ibid., 14.
17. Ibid., 12.
18. Ibid., 15.
19. Ibid.
20. Ibid., 30, 31.
21. Neal McLeod, *Cree Narrative Memory: From Treaties to Contemporary Times* (Saskatoon, SK: Purich Pub. Ltd., 2007), 70.
22. Ibid., 18.
23. Karl Rahner, "On the Theology of Hope," in *Theological Investigations, Vol. 10*, trans. David Bourke (New York: Herder & Herder, 1973), 242–51.
24. Allen Jorgenson, "Rahner, Romans and Suffering Hope," *Toronto Journal of Theology* 21, no. 2 (2005): 184.
25. See Karl Rahner, "Anonymous Christians," in *Theological Investigation, Vol. 6*, trans. Karl-H. and Boniface Kruger (London: Darton, Longman and Todd, 1969), 390–98.
26. Jorgenson, "Suffering Hope," 184.
27. Ibid., 186.
28. Aquinas is among the first of the Western Christian theologians who made use of the re-introduction of Aristotle to the west by Muslim scholars. Aristotle, in his famous *Nichomachean Ethics*, described the virtues as those human actions whereby we make something of ourselves. Aquinas took this idea and gave it a twist when he thought about faith, hope, and love.
29. Pamela R. McCarroll, *Waiting at the Foot of the Cross: Toward a Theology of Hope for Today* (Eugene, OR: Wipf and Stock, 2013), 191.
30. See Luther, LW 31, 52, 53: "'For since, in the wisdom of God, the world did not know God through wisdom, it pleased God through the folly of what we preach to save those who believe.' Now it is not sufficient for anyone, and it does him no good to recognize God in his glory and majesty, unless he recognizes him in the humility and shame of the cross."
31. Richard Kearney and James Taylor, "Introduction," in *Hosting the Stranger: Between Religions*, eds. Richard Kearney and James Taylor (New York: Continuum Intl Pub Group, 2011), 1.
32. Randy Woodley, "Native American Hospitality and Generosity," in *Strangers in this World: Multireligious Reflections on Immigration*, eds. Hussam S. Timani, Allen G. Jorgenson, and Alexander Y. Hwang (Minneapolis, MN: Fortress Press, 2015), 186.
33. Woodley, "Native American Hospitality and Generosity," 189. See also Terry LeBlanc, "Walking in Reconciled Relationships," *Consensus* 37, no. 1 (2016), Article 4, http://scholars.wlu.ca/consensus/vol37/iss1/4.
34. Jacques Derrida, *Acts of Religion*, trans. Gil Anidjar (New York: Routledge, 2010), 362.
35. See ibid., 380 where he notes that it is impossible to be a guest or host both without the practice of forgiveness, for our imposition on the other and for our failure to be what is needed.
36. See Aldred, "A Shared Narrative," 193–206.

37. Louise Bernice Halfe, "Dedication to the Seventh Generation," Poetry London, accessed March 28, 2020, https://poetrylondon.ca/louise-bernice-halfe/.

38. Susan Neylan, *The Heavens Are Changing* (Montreal and Kingston: McGill-Queen's University Press, 2003), 6.

39. Ibid., 8–9.

40. Ibid., 15.

41. Sarah J. King, *Fishing in Contested Waters: Place and Community in Burnt Church/Esgenoopetitj* (Toronto: University of Toronto Press, 2014), 101–104.

42. Kidwell et al., *A Native American Theology*, 32.

43. See "Religious Plurality and Christian Self Understanding," World Council of Churches, January 1, 2004, https://www.oikoumene.org/en/resources/documents/commissions/faith-and-order/ix-other-study-processes/religious-plurality-and-christian-self-understanding.

44. Ibid., 10.

45. Ibid., 12.

46. Ibid.

47. Ibid., 14.

48. Ibid., 5.

49. Ibid., 6.

50. Ibid., 5.

51. Ibid. See also Peter C. Phan, "Multiple Religious Belonging: Opportunities and Challenges for Theology and Church," *Theological Studies* 64, no. 3 (September 1, 2003): 505–513.

52. Even religious communities that ignore one another in a situation of pluralism say something about themselves or the other by that very act.

53. Woodley, *Shalom and the Community of Creation*, 81.

54. Wilson, *Research Is Ceremony*, 73.

55. WCC, "Religious Plurality," 15.

56. See Daniel Maoz and Allen Jorgenson, "Teaching Exodus Interreligiously," in *Teaching Interreligious Encounters*, eds. Marc A. Pugliese and Alexander Y. Hwang (New York: Oxford University Press, 2017), 182–185.

57. Thatamanil, "Eucharist Upstairs, Yoga Downstairs," 6.

58. "Rabbi" here is understood in the simple sense of being a teacher, and not after the contemporary manner of a leader of a synagogue, which would be anachronistic.

59. See 88 above.

60. Johnston, *Ojibway Heritage*, 43. See also Monture, *We Share Our Matters*, 168.

61. "Traditional Tobacco," Keep it Sacred: National Native Network, accessed December 17, 2018, https://keepitsacred.itcmi.org/tobacco-and-tradition/traditional-tobacco-use/.

62. Aldred, "A Shared Narrative," 202.

63. Allen G. Jorgenson, *Awe and Expectation: On Being Stewards of the Gospel* (Eugene, OR: Wipf & Stock, 2010), 12.

Bibliography

Aldred, Ray. "Freedom: A Cree Theologian's Account." Lecture presented at Waterloo Lutheran Seminary, Wilfrid Laurier University, November 12, 2012.

———. "A Shared Narrative." In *Strangers in This World: Multireligious Reflections on Immigration,* edited by Hussam S. Timani, Allen G. Jorgenson, and Alexander Y. Hwang, 193–206. Minneapolis: Fortress Press, 2015.

Alfred, Taiaike. *Peace, Power and Righteousness: An Indigenous Manifesto,* 2nd ed. Oxford: Oxford University Press, 2009.

Amore, Roy T C. and Amil Hussain. "About Religion." In *A Concise Introduction to World Religions: Third Edition,* edited by Willard G. Oxtoby, Roy C. Amore, Amir Hussain, and Alan F. Segal, 2–29. Oxford: Oxford University Press, 2015.

Anttila, Miikka E. "Music." In *Engaging Luther: A (New) Theological Assessment,* edited by Olli-Pekka Vainio. Eugene, OR: Cascade Books, 2010.

Aristotle. *On the Nature of the Soul,* translated by W. S. Hett. Harvard, MA: Harvard University Press, 1995.

Bachelard, Gaston. *The Poetics of Space: The Classic Look At How We Experience Intimate Places,* translated by Maria Jolas. Boston, MA: Beacon Press, 1958.

Bauer, Walter, William F. Arndt, F. Wilbur Gingrich, and Frederick W. Danker, eds. "Kairos." In *A Greek-English Lexicon of the New Testament and Other Early Christian Literature Second Edition,* 394, 395. Chicago: University of Chicago Press, 1979.

Becker, Jean. "Untitled." Lecture, Wilfrid Laurier University, Waterloo, Ontario February 2011.

Beyer, Peter. *Religions and Global Society.* Abingdon: Routledge, 2006.

Bhabha, Homi K. *The Location of Culture.* London: Routledge, 2004.

Bowker, John. "Religion." In *Oxford Concise Dictionary of World Religions,* edited by John Bowker. Oxford: Oxford University Press, 2005.

Brueggemann, Walter. *The Land: Place as Gift, Promise, and Challenge in Biblical Faith Second Edition.* Minneapolis, MN: Fortress Press, 2002.

Buechner, Frederick. *The Sacred Journey: A Memoir of Early Days.* New York: Harper Collins, 1991.
Cardinal, Harold. "Okimaw Win and Post-colonial Nation-Building." In *Intersecting Voices: Critical Theologies in a Land of Diversity*, edited by Don Schweitzer and Derek Simon, 192–199. Toronto: Novalis Press, 2004.
Cardinal, Harold and W. Hildebrandt. *Treaty Elders of Saskatchewan: Our Dream is That Our People Will One Day be Clearly Recognized as Nations.* Calgary: University of Calgary Press, 2000.
CBC. "Government Apologies for Residential Schools in 2008." Last updated June 25, 2018. https://www.cbc.ca/archives/government-apologizes-for-residential-schools-in-2008-1.4666041
Chung, Paul S., Ulrich Duchrow, and Craig Nessan. *Liberating Lutheran Theology: Freedom for Justice and Solidarity with Others in a Global Context.* Minneapolis, MN: Fortress Press, 2011.
Clooney, S.J., Francis X., ed. *The New Comparative Theology: Interreligious Insights from the Next Generation.* London: T&T Clark, 2003.
Cresswell, Tim. *Place: An Introduction*, 2nd ed. Malden, MA: Wiley Blackwell, 2015.
Crozier, Lorna. "Afterword." In *The Poetry of Lorna Crozier*, edited by Catherine Hunter, 55–60. Waterloo: WLU Press, 2005.
Daschuk, James. *Clearing the Plains: Disease, Politics of Starvation, and the Loss of Aboriginal Life.* Regina: University of Regina Press, 2013.
Dellinger, Lisa A. "Sin–Ambiguity and Complexity and the Sin of Not Conforming." In *Coming Full Circle: Constructing Native Christian Theology*, edited by Steven Charleston and Elaine. A. Robinson, 119–132. Minneapolis: Fortress Press, 2015.
Deloria Jr., Vine, *Custer Died for Your Sins: An Indian Manifesto.* Norman: Oklahoma University Press, 1988.
———. *God Is Red: A Native View of Religion.* Golden, CO: Fulcrum Pub., 2003.
Derrida, Jacques. *Acts of Religion*, translated by Gil Anidjar. New York: Routledge, 2010.
———. *On Cosmopolitanism and Forgiveness*, translated by Mark Dooley and Michael Hughes. London: Routledge, 1997.
Eliade, Mircea. *The Sacred and Profane: The Nature of Religion.* Boston, MA: Mariner Book 2001.
Erdrich, Heid E. "The Theft Outright." Poetry Foundation. Accessed March 28, 2020. https://www.poetryfoundation.org/poems/89050/the-theft-outright.
Erdrich, Louise E. "Indian Boarding School: The Runaways." Poetry Foundation. Accessed March 27, 2020. https://www.poetryfoundation.org/poems/43079/indian-boarding-school-the-runaways
Fenton, William N. *The Great Law and the Longhouse: A Political History of the Iroquois Confederacy.* Norman: University of Oklahoma Press, 1998.
Feuerbach, Ludwig. *The Essence of Christianity*, edited by George Eliot. Buffalo, NY: Prometheus Books, 1989.
Ford, David. *Shaping Theology: Engagements in a Religious and Secular World.* Malden, MA: Blackwell Publishing, 2007.

Gerle, Elisabeth. *Passionate Embrace: Luther on Love, Body and Sensual Presence.* Eugene: OR, Cascade, 2017.

Goris, Wouter and Jan Aertsen. "Medieval Theories of Transcendentals." In *Stanford Encyclopedia of Philosophy (Online).* Accessed August 28, 2018. https://plato.stanford.edu/entries/transcendentals-medieval/.

Gregersen, Niels Henrik, Bengt Kristensson Uggla, and Trygve Wyller, eds. *Reformation Theology for a Post-Secular Age: Løgstrup, Prenter, Wingren, and the Future of Scandinavian Creation Theology.* Göttingen: Vandenhoek & Ruprecht, 2017.

Griffiths, Rudyard, ed. *Our Story: Aboriginal Voices on Canada's Past.* Toronto: Anchor Canada, 2004.

Gustafson, Hans. "Descandalizing Multiple Religious Identity with Help from Nicholas Black Elk and His Spirituality: An Exercise in Interreligious Learning." *Journal of Ecumenical Studies* 51, no. 1 (Winter 2016): 80–113.

Halfe, Louise Bernice. "Dedication to the Seventh Generation." Poetry London. Accessed March 28, 2020. https://poetrylondon.ca/louise-bernice-halfe/.

Hannon, Gerald. "The Pink Indian." *Toronto Life,* September, 2011, 56–62.

Harjo, Joy. Conflict Resolution for Holy Beings." Poetry Foundation. Accessed March 30, 2020. https://www.poetryfoundation.org/poems/141847/conflict-resolution-for-holy-beings.

Heaney, Seamus. *Field Work: Poems.* New York: Farrar, 1976.

Heim, S. Mark. *Salvations: Truth and Difference in Religion.* Maryknoll, NY: Orbis, 1995.

———. *The Depth of the Riches: A Trinitarian Theology of Religious Ends.* Grand Rapids, MI: Eerdmans, 2001.

Helmer, Christine. *How Luther Became the Reformer.* Louisville, KY: Westminster/John Knox, 2019.

———. *The Trinity and Martin Luther: Revised Edition.* Bellingham, WA: Lexham Press, 2017.

Johnston, Basil. *Ojibway Heritage.* Toronto: McClelland and Stewart, 1976.

———. *The Manitous.* St. Paul: The Minnesota Historical Society, 2001.

Jorgenson, Allen G. *Awe and Expectation: On Being Stewards of the Gospel.* Eugene, OR: Wipf & Stock, 2010.

———. "Empire, Eschatology and Stolen Land." *Dialogue* 49, no. 2 (Summer 2010): 115–22.

———. "Immigrants as *Terra* Nullius: On the Need for a Comparative Theology of Decolonization." In *The Meaning of my Neighbor's Faith,* edited by Alexander Y. Hwang and Laura E. Alexander. Lanham, MD: Lexington Books/Fortress Press, 2019.

———. "Rahner, Romans and Suffering Hope," *Toronto Journal of Theology* 21, no. 2 (2005): 183–98.

———. *The Appeal to Experience in the Christologies of Friedrich Schleiermacher and Karl Rahner.* New York: Peter Lang, 2007.

Jorgenson, Allen G., Mona Tokarek LaFosse, Debbie Lou Ludolph, and Mary (Joy) Philip. "Respecting Indigenous Spirituality in its Own Right." Panel at Canadian Theological Society, Regina, SK, May 28, 2018.

Kant, Immanuel. "An Answer to the Question: What Is Enlightenment?" In *Practical Philosophy, The Cambridge Edition of the Works of Immanuel Kant*, edited by Mary J. Gregor. Cambridge: Cambridge University Press, 1996.

———. *Religion Within the Limits of Reason Alone*, edited by Theodore M. Greene and Hoyt H. Hudson. New York: Harper, 1960.

Kearney, Richard and Brian Treanor (eds.). *Carnal Hermeneutics*. New York: Fordham, 2015.

Kearney, Richard and James Taylor. "Introduction." In *Hosting the Stranger: Between Religions*, edited by Richard Kearney and James Taylor, 1–8. New York: Continuum Intl Pub Group, 2011.

Keep it Sacred: National Native Network, "Traditional Tobacco." Accessed December 17, 2018. https://keepitsacred.itcmi.org/tobacco-and-tradition/traditional-tobacco-use

Keller, Catherine. *Political Theology of the Earth: Our Planetary Emergency and the Struggle for a New Republic*. New York: Columbia University Press, 2018.

Kidwell, Clara Sue, Homer Noley, and George Tinker E. *A Native American Theology*. New York: Orbis Books, 2002.

King, Sarah J. *Fishing in Contested Waters: Place and Community in Burnt Church/Esgenoopetitj*. Toronto: University of Toronto Press, 2014.

King, Thomas. *The Truth About Stories: A Native Narrative*. Toronto: Anansi Press, 2003.

Koning, Robin. "Walking the Land: Inculturation and Footprints in the Western Desert of Australia." *Toronto Journal of Theology* 21, no. 1 (Spring 2005): 91–104.

Kovach, Margaret. *Indigenous Methodologies: Characteristics, Conversations, and Contexts*. Toronto: University of Toronto Press, 2009.

LaFosse, Mona Tokarek. "Those Who Hear: The Power of Learners in 1 Timothy." In *Religions and Education in Antiquity: Studies in Honour of Michel Desjardins*, edited by Alex Damm, 147–70. Leiden: Brill, 2019.

Lamm, Julia A. *The Living God: Schleiermacher's Theological Appropriation of Spinoza*. University Park, PA: The Pennsylvania State University Press, 1996.

Laugrand, Frédéric B. and Jarich G. Oosten, *Inuit Shamanism and Christianity: Transitions and Transformations in the Twentieth Century*. Montreal and Kingston: McGill-Queen's University Press, 2010.

LeBlanc, Terry. "Walking in Reconciled Relationships." *Consensus* 37, no. (2016), Article 4. http://scholars.wlu.ca/consensus/vol37/iss1/4.

Leith, John H, ed. *Creeds of the Churches*, 3rd ed. Louisville, KY: Anchor Books, 1982.

Lindbeck, George. *The Nature of Doctrine: Religious and Theology in a Postliberal Age*. Philadelphia, PA: The Westminster Press, 1984.

Løgstrup, Knut. *The Ethical Demand*, Introduction by Hans Fink and Alasdair MacIntyre, various translators. Notre Dame, IN: University of Notre Dame Press, 1997.

Longboat, Dan. "Hodinohso:ni Ecological Knowledge and the Dish with One Spoon Conversation in Cultural Fluency #2 Conference," YouTube, October, 2015. https://www.youtube.com/watch?v=e5szQHeQ9FM.

Luther, Martin. *Luther's Works, American Edition, 55 Volumes*, edited by Jaroslav Pelikan (vols. 1–30) and Helmut Lehmann (vols. 31–55). Philadelphia, PA: Fortress and St. Louis: Concordia, 1955–86.
Lyotard, Jean-François. *The Post-Modern Explained*. Minneapolis: University of Minnesota Press, 1992.
MacDonald, Bishop Mark. "Day of Dialogue." Lecture presented at Waterloo Lutheran Seminary, November 3, 2011.
MacGregor, Geddes M. *Dictionary of Religion and Philosophy*. New York: Paragon House, 1991.
Maoz, Daniel and Allen Jorgenson. "Teaching Exodus Interreligiously." In *Teaching Interreligious Encounters*, edited by Marc A. Pugliese and Alexander Y. Hwang, 182–185. New York: Oxford University Press, 2017.
Marshall, Bruce. *Trinity and Truth*. Cambridge: Cambridge University Press, 2000.
McCarroll, Pamela R. *Waiting at the Foot of the Cross: Toward a Theology of Hope for Today*. Eugene, OR: Wipf and Stock, 2013.
McLeod, Neal. *Cree Narrative Memory: From Treaties to Contemporary Times*. Saskatoon, SK: Purich Pub. Ltd., 2007.
Michaels, Anne. *Fugitive Pieces*. Toronto: McClelland and Stewart Inc., 1996.
Moïsi, Dominique. *The Geopolitics of Emotion: How Cultures of Fear, Humiliation and Hope are Reshaping the World*. New York: Anchor, 2010.
Monture, Rick. *We Share our Matters: Two Centuries of Writing and Resistance at Six Nations of the Grand River*. Winnipeg: University of Manitoba Press, 2014.
Neylan, Susan. *The Heavens Are Changing*. Montreal and Kingston: McGill-Queen's University Press, 2003.
Nicolson, Hugh. *Comparative Theology and the Problem of Religious Rivalry*. Oxford: Oxford University Press, 2011.
Ohlson, Kristen. *Stalking the Divine: Contemplating Faith with the Poor Claires*. New York: Hachette Books, 2003.
Orsi, Robert A. *History and Presence*. Cambridge, MA: The Belknap Press of Harvard University Press, 2016.
Pedersen, Else Marie Wiberg, ed. *The Alternative Luther: Lutheran Theology from the Subaltern*. Lanham, MD: Lexington/Fortress, 2019.
Peelman, Achiel. "The Meeting of the Rivers: Being Native and Christian in Canada." *Toronto Journal of Theology* 21, no. 1 (Spring 2005): 15–32.
Peiter, Hermann. *Christliche Ethik bei Schleiermacher – Christian Ethics according to Schleiermacher: Gesammelte Afsätze und Besprechungen – Collected Essays and Reviews*, edited by Terrence N. Tice. Eugene, OR: Wipf and Stock, 2010.
Pétrement, Simone. *Simone Weil: A Life*, translated by Raymond Rosenthal. New York: Pantheon Books, 1976.
Phan, Peter C. "Multiple Religious Belonging: Opportunities and Challenges for Theology and Church." *Theological Studies* 64, no. 3 (September 1, 2003): 505–513.
Philip, Mary (Joy). "Remembrance." In *Churrasco: A Theological Feast in Honor of Vítor Westhelle*, edited by Mary Philip, John Arthur Nunes, and Charles M. Collier, 94–104. Eugen, OR: Pickwick, 2013.

———. "The Space In Between Spaces: The Church as Prophetic Pest/Parasite." In *Being the Church in the Midst of Empire: Trinitarian Reflections*, edited by Karen L. Bloomquist, 91–106. Minneapolis, MN: Lutheran University Press, 2007.

Prenter, Regin. *Spiritus Creator,* translated by John M. Jensen. Eugene, OR: 2001.

Race, Alan and Paul Hedges, eds. *Christian Approaches to Other Faiths.* London: SCM Press, 2008.

Rahner, S.J., Karl. "Anonymous Christians." In *Theological Investigation, Volume 6,* translated by Karl-H. and Boniface Kruger, 390–398. London: Darton, Longman and Todd, 1969.

———. "On the Theology of Hope." In *Theological Investigations, Volume 10,* translated by David Bourke, 242–251. New York: Herder & Herder, 1973.

———. *Schriften zur Theologie IX.* Zürich: Benzinger, 1970.

Rajkumar, Peniel Jesudason Rufus and Joseph Prabhakar Dayam, eds. *Many Yet One? Multiple Religious Belonging.* Geneva: World Council of Churches.

Reid, Jennifer. "The Doctrine of Discovery and Canadian Law." *Canadian Journal of Native Studies* 30, no. 3 (2010): 335–359.

Rhoads, David, Joanna Dewey and Donald Michie. *Mark as Story: Introduction to the Narrative of a Gospel, Third Edition.* Minneapolis, MN: Fortress Press, 2012.

Ross, Rupert. *Dancing with a Ghost: Exploring Aboriginal Reality.* Toronto: Penguin, 2006.

Saskatchewan History and Folklore Society. "Fort Walsh to Wood Mountain – North West Mounted Police Trail." Accessed July 2, 2020. http://www.shfs.ca/trails

Saul, John Ralston. *A Fair Country: Telling Truths About Canada.* Toronto: Viking Canada, 2008.

Savage, Candace. *A Geography of Blood: Unearthing Memory from a Prairie Landscape.* Toronto: Greystone Books, 2012.

Schleiermacher, Friedrich. *Christian Faith: A New Translation and Critical Edition,* translated and edited by Terrence N. Tice, Catherine L. Kelsey, and Edwina Lawler. Louisville, KY: Westminster John Knox Press, 2016.

———. *Dialectics, or, the Art of Doing Philosophy: A Study Ed. Of the 1811 Notes,* translated by Terrence N. Tice. Atlanta: Scholars Press, 1998.

———. *Lectures on Philosophical Ethics,* translated by Louise Adey Huish. Cambridge: Cambridge University Press, 2002.

———. *On the Doctrine of Election with Special Reference to the* Aphorisms *of Dr. Bretschneider,* translated by Iain G. Nicol and Allen G. Jorgenson. Louisville, KY: Westminster John Knox Press, 2011.

———. *On the* Glaubenslehre*: Two Letters to Dr. Lücke,* translated by James Duke and Francis Fiorenza. Chico, CA: Scholar's Press, 1981.

———. *On Religion: Speeches to the Cultured Despisers,* edited and translated by Richard Crouter. Cambridge: Cambridge University Press, 1996.

———. *Reformed but Ever Reforming: Sermons in Relation to the Celebration of the Handing Over of the Augsburg Confession (1830),* translated by Iain G. Nicol. Lewiston: The Edwin Mellen Press, 1997.

———. *Sämmtliche Werke II,2.* Berlin: G. Reimer, 1821.

———. *Schleiermacher's Soliloquies*, translated by Horace Leland Friess. Chicago: Open Court, 1926.
Sharma, Arvind. "Reciprocal Illumination." In *Interreligious Comparisons in Religious Studies and Theology*, edited by Perry Schmidt-Leukel and Andreas Nehring, 178–90. New York: Bloomsbury, 2016.
Simpson, Leanne. "Decolonial Love, Indigenous Resurgence and the Art of Living Justly." Lecture presented at Wilfrid Laurier University, Waterloo, ON, December 2, 2015.
Six Nations of the Grand River Nation. "Six Miles Deep: Land Rights of the Six Nations of the Grand River." Accessed March 08, 2020. http://www.sixnations.ca/SixMilesDeepBooklet2015Final.pdf.
Smith, Jonathan Z. *Divine Drudgery: On the Comparison of Early Christianities and the Religions of Late Antiquity*. Chicago: University of Chicago Press, 1990.
Soja, Edward W. *Postmodern Geographies: The Reassertion of Space in Critical Social Theory*. New York: Verso, 1989.
Sorabji, Richard. *Aristotle on Memory*, 2nd ed. Chicago: University of Chicago Press, 2004.
Spivak, Gayatri Chakravorty. *A Critique of Postcolonial Reason: Toward a History of the Vanishing Present*. Cambridge, MA: Harvard University Press, 1999.
———. "Can the Subaltern Speak?" In *Can the Subaltern Speak: Reflections on the History of an Idea*, edited by Rosalind Morris, 21–78. New York: Columbia University Press, 2010.
Stayer, James M. *Martin Luther: German Saviour: German Evangelical Theological Factions and the Interpretation of Luther, 1917-1933*. Montreal and Kingston: McGill-Queens University Press, 2000.
Streufert, Mary J., ed. *Transformative Lutheran Theologies: Feminist, Womanist, and Mujerista Perspectives*. Minneapolis, MN: Fortress Press, 2010.
Tanner, Kathryn. "Eschatology and Ethics." In *The Oxford Handbook of Theological Ethics*, edited by Gilbert Meilaender and William Werpehowski, 41–56. Oxford: Oxford University Press, 2005.
Taylor, Charles. *A Secular Age*. Cambridge, MA.: Harvard University Press, 2007.
Taylor, Drew Hayden. *Motorcycles and Sweetgrass: A Novel*. Toronto: Knopf, 2010.
The Canadian Encyclopedia. "Cypress Hills." Accessed December 12, 2018. https://www.thecanadianencyclopedia.ca/en/article/cypress-hills.
Thompson, Deanna. *Crossing the Divide: Luther, Feminism, and the Cross*. Minneapolis, MN: Fortress Press, 2004.
Tice, Terrence. *Abingdon Pillars of Theology: Schleiermacher*. Nashville, TN: Abingdon Press, 2006.
Tillich Paul. "Art and Ultimate Reality." In *Art, Creativity, and the Sacred*, edited by Diane Apostolos-Cappadona. New York: Continuum, 1998.
Timani, Hussam S., Allen G. Jorgenson, and Alexander Y. Hwang, eds. *Strangers in This World: Multireligious Reflection on Immigration*. Minneapolis, MN: Fortress Press, 2015.
Tinker, George "Tink". *A Native American Theology*. Maryknoll, NY: Orbis Press, 2001.

———. *American Indian Liberation: A Theology of Sovereignty*. Maryknoll, NY: Orbis Books, 2008.

Tranströmer, Tomas, *The Deleted World: Poems*, versions by Robin Robertson. Toronto: Anansi Press, 2011.

Trelstad, Marit. "Charity Terror Begins at Home: Luther and the 'Terrifying and Killing' Law." In *Lutherrenaisance Past and Present,* edited by Christine Helmer and Bo Kristian Holm, 209–23. Göttingen: Vandenhoeck & Ruprecht, 2015.

Truth and Reconciliation Commission of Canada. *They Came for the Children: Canada, Aboriginal Peoples, and Residential Schools.* Winnipeg: Truth and Reconciliation Commission of Canada, 2012.

Tweed, Thomas. *Crossing and Dwelling: A Theory of Religion.* Cambridge, MA: Harvard, 2008.

United Nations Declaration on the Rights of Indigenous Peoples, United Nations. Accessed August 28, 2018. https://www.un.org/esa/socdev/unpfii/documents/DRIPS_en.pdf

Voss Roberts, Michelle. "Religious Belonging and the Multiple." *Journal of Feminist Studies in Religion* 26, no. 1 (2010): 43–62.

Westhelle, Vítor. *Eschatology and Space*. New York: Palgrave MacMillan, 2012.

———. "Liberation Theology: A Latitudinal Perspective." In *The Oxford Handbook of Eschatology,* edited by Jerry L. Walls, 311–27. Oxford: Oxford University Press, 2008.

Wiebe, Rudy. *Big Bear*. Toronto: Penguin Canada, 2008.

Wilson, Shawn. *Research Is Ceremony: Indigenous Research Methods*. Winnipeg: Fernwood, 2008.

Wingren, Gustaf. *Credo: The Christian View of Faith and Life*, translated by Edgar M. Carlson. Minneapolis, MN: Augsburg, 1981.

———. *Creation and Gospel*. Toronto, ON: Edwin Mellen Press, 1979.

———. Creation and Law, translated by Ross McKenzie. (Eugene, OR: Wipf and Stock, 2003).

Woodley, Randy S. *Shalom and the Community of Creation: An Indigenous Vision*. Grand Rapids, MI: William B. Eerdmans Pub. Co., 2012.

World Council of Churches. "Religious Plurality and Christian Self Understanding." January 1, 2004. https://www.oikoumene.org/en/resources/documents/commissions/faith-and-order/ix-other-study-processes/religious-plurality-and-christian-self-understanding.

Index

aboriginal. *See* Indigenous
Absolon, Kathy, xv
Aldred, Ray, 7, 76, 88
Alfred, Taiaike, 9, 44
Aristotle, 52n20, 91n28
art, xxviin31, 44–45, 47–48, 50, 52n16

Bachelard, Gaston, 26, 36n34
baptism, 12, 29, 63, 87
Barth, Karl, xiv, xxvinn14–15, 25–26, 38
Beyer, Peter, xxvn3
borders, xxiii, 13–15, 20n66, 78, 84
boundary, boundaries, xix, xxvn3, 13–16, 45, 67, 77, 83
Bowker, John, xxvn3
Brueggemann, Walter, 7
Buechner, Frederick, xiii

Cardinal, Harold, xix
Christ, Jesus: and being human, 27; and communion, 88; and creation, 27, 69–70; and death, 57–58, 63, 65, 70; and new creation, 4, 62–65, 69–70; and resurrection, 10, 28, 63, 69, 73n15; and salvation, 28, 39, 85
Chung, Paul S., 34n6
circle, xv–xvii, 10, 22–23, 48–49, 55
Clooney, Francis X., xviii

communion. *See* Eucharist
community, xv, xxi, 4, 7–9, 12, 14–16, 22, 30–31, 44–45, 55–56, 58–59, 61, 67, 71
comparative theology, xii–xiii, xxviin33, 12, 59–60, 72, 73n19; as autobiographical, xiii–xv; as circular, xv–xvii; as ethical-political, xvii–xx; as generative, xx–xxii; and truth, xx–xxiii
creation, xi, xvi, xxiii–xxiv, 4, 6, 9, 12, 14, 22–27, 29–33, 55, 59, 61–65, 85–86, 88; as giving birth, xxiv, 6, 61, 69, 75
Creator, xix, xxixn58, 6, 8, 11–17, 23–24, 26, 46, 50, 61, 64, 88
Cresswell, Tim, xxixn65
cross, 57, 62–63, 65, 69–70, 73n13, 75, 81, 91n30
Crozier, Lorna, 33
crucify, crucifixion, xxviin32, 63, 73n15

Daschuk, James, 90n2
death, dying, 57–58, 62–65, 69–70, 73n5
Deloria Jr., Vine, xxiii, 1–7, 14, 17, 17n7, 18n9, 21, 63
Derrida, Jacques, 82–83
Doctrine of Discovery, 46

Duchrow, Ulrich, 34n6

earth: as agent, 5–7, 69; as mother, xxiv, xxixn58, 6, 9, 18n17, 59, 61, 69–70, 75, 77
Eliade, Mircea, xv, xxii
Enlightenment, xii, xvii, 1, 10, 53n45
eschatology, *eschatos*, xvi, 16, 64
ethics, xxvn3, 30, 33, 43–45, 47, 60
Eucharist, 88–89
evil, 10–13, 28, 58, 64–65. *See also* sin
exegesis, xxviiin56, 66–68

faith, 24, 27, 31, 47, 56, 73n13, 81, 85–86, 89, 91n28
Fenton, William N., 35n7
Feuerbach, Ludwig, xiv
First Nations: and the Americas, xi–xii, xix, 6–8, 13, 17n7, 58–59; and diversity, 9–10, 59–60, 72, 85; and hospitality, 45–46, 68, 82–83, 89; and residential schools, xix, xxviiin52, xxixn58, 3, 17n7, 65; and spirituality, xv, xviii–xxi, xxviiin48, 5–6, 14, 20n66, 48–49, 76–77, 88–89. *See also* Indigenous

gospel, xiv, 3–5, 21–24, 26–27, 32, 34n4, 34n6, 56, 70

harmony, xiii, xvi, xxiv, 11, 13, 17, 32–34, 40, 42, 46, 48–51, 55, 59, 64
Heim, S. Mark, xviii
Helmer, Christine, 34n6, 35n15, 36n29
hermeneutic, hermeneutical, xvii, xx–xxi, xxiii, xxviin33, 34n6, 38, 87
Hildebrandt, W., xix
hope, xxiv, 56, 65, 69, 72, 77–81, 83, 86, 88–90
hospitality, xxiv, 45, 51, 68, 73n19, 82, 85, 87, 89. *See also* place, non-competitive
hunting, 9, 59, 66–67

Indigenous: and community, 7–9, 12, 14, 59, 61, 86–87; and individuality, 7–8; and land, xix, 3, 5–8, 14–16, 40, 46, 58–59, 76–77, 82, 88–89; and language, xxi, xxixn58, 8–9; and original sanctity, 10–13, 28, 64; and place, xxiii–xxiv, 5–7, 14–17, 32, 45–46, 48, 55, 58–59, 69, 76–77, 79–80; and ritual, xxii–xxiii, xxviiin48, 9, 11–12, 84, 88–89; and time, xv–xvi, 10–11. *See also* First Nations
interreligious encounter, xv, xxiv, xxvin7, 60, 82–88
Inuit, 6, 67
Irenaeus, 26–27

Jew, Jewish, Judaism, 3, 10, 12–13, 68, 88
Johnston, Basil, 5, 10, 13, 16, 57, 69–70

Kant, Immanuel, xvii, xxiv, xxvn5, 40, 43, 47
Keller, Catherine, 78
Kidwell, Clara Sue, xv
King, Sarah J., 84
King, Thomas, xxi, 8, 13–14
Kovach, Margaret, xv, 90n6

LaFosse, Mona Tokarek, xxviiin56
land: and Christianity, xxiii, 1–3, 6–7, 17, 30; and circularity, 11–13; as mother, xxiv, xxixn58, 6, 9, 18n17, 59, 61, 69–70, 75, 77; and relationship, xxiv, 14, 27, 64, 71; and settlers, xi, xix, xxiii, 15, 34n3, 46, 68; and spirituality, xxiii, xxixn58, 76, 88–89; and stories, 5–6, 8, 15, 32, 82. *See also* Indigenous, and land
law: and gospel, 4, 21–24, 26, 34n4, 34n6; and the Great Law of Peace, 25; and love, 25
liminality. *See* margins
Lindbeck, George, 38
Løgstrup, Knud, 26, 30, 32
Longboat, Dan, xiii
Lord's Supper. *See* Eucharist
love, xiv, xxiv, xxvin15, 24–25, 71, 75, 79, 81, 88, 91n28

Luther, 21, 23–25, 34n6, 35n15, 56, 58, 67–68, 81; and body, 27–28; and creation, xxiii–xxiv, 22, 26–27, 29–30; and the Holy Spirit, 29, 31–33, 55; and kenosis, 29–32; and music, 31, 36n33, 66; and Scripture, 31–32, 66–68; and sin, 24, 28–29

MacDonald, Bishop Mark, 22
Manitou, 5, 14–15; Kitchi-Manitou, 5–6, 15–16, 69
margins: and hope, xxiv, 77, 81–83, 88–90; and interfaith encounter, xxiv, 72, 77–78, 83; in relation to the center, 15, 57, 82; as revelatory, 72, 77, 82
McCarroll, Pamela R., 81
McLeod, Neal, 79–80
method, methodology, xii, xv–xvi, 72
Michaels, Anne, 58
migration, 45
Moïsi, Dominique, xxiv, 78–79
Monture, Rick, 24–25, 35n7

Native. *See* Indigenous
Nessan, Craig, 34n6
Neylan, Susan, 84
Nicolson, Hugh, xx, xxii
Noley, Homer, xv

Ohlson, Kristen, xxviin31
orality, xix, xxi, xxviiin56, 8, 80
original sanctity, 10–13, 28, 64

Peacemaker, 24–25, 35n7
Pedersen, Else Marie Wiberg, 34n6
Peelman, Achiel, 20n66
Philip, Mary (Joy), 18n17
pilgrimage, xv, xxvin7, 71, 73n19, 75–76
place: harmonic, xxiv, 37–51; kairotic, xxiii–xxiv, 16–17, 33, 51, 55, 63, 69–72, 75, 88–89; kenotic, xxiv, 22, 29–33; and margins, xxiv, 16, 63, 77, 81–83, 89; non-competitive, xxiv, 46, 51, 70–72; and time, xvi, xxiii, 1, 16, 64, 66. *See also* margins; space
Pöder, Christine Svinth-Værge, 35n22
poetry, 31–33, 36n34, 51, 57; as indirect discourse, 32–33, 69, 72; revelatory potential, 69, 71–72
Prenter, Regin, 26, 29, 35n22

Rahner, Karl, xiv–xv, xxiv, 80–81
Reign of God, xxiv, 4, 51, 68
religion: and art, xxviin31, 47–48, 50; and comparative theology, xii, xvii–xviii, xx, xxii; defining, xxvn3, xxviiin48; and Indigenous practices, xix-xx, xxviiin48, 20n66, 84; interreligious encounter, xxiv, xxvin7, 60, 83–84, 87–88; and land, xxiii, 1–2, 4, 6–7; plurality, xviii, 59, 77, 83–86; and Schleiermacher, 37, 39, 47–48, 50, 54n48
residential schools, xxviiin52, xxixn58, 3, 17n7, 65
Ross, Rupert, 8, 11, 28–29

Savage, Candace, 76, 90n2
Schleiermacher, 18n29, 53n45, 73n15; and art, 47–48, 50, 52n16; critique, 37–39; and ethics, 43–45; and feeling, 37, 40, 42, 48; and intuition, 47–48, 50, 54n48; and language, 38; and place and space, 17, 42–46, 50–51, 52n24, 55; and thought, 40–41, 43; and time, 42, 52n24; and truth, 40–43; and universal, 44, 48, 52n16, 54n48
scripture, xxi–xxii, xxviiin56, 9, 12, 31–32, 61, 73n13
Sharma, Arvind, xxii
Simpson, Leanne, xv
sin, xii, 10, 12–13, 24, 27–29, 58, 61, 64–65, 73n15, 79, 89
Six Nations, xi, xxvn1, 24, 35n9
Soja, Edward W., xxviin27, xxixn65
space: and being, 5, 16, 36n34, 42, 47, 49, 52n24; and creation, xxiv, 4, 6, 18n9, 26–27, 69–70; as distinguished

from land and place, 3, 5, 43; and freedom, 15–16, 56–57; kairotic, xxiii–xxiv, 16–17, 33, 51, 55, 63, 69–72, 75, 88–89; kenotic, xxiv, 22, 29–33; and narrative, 5–6, 10, 49, 80, 82; non-competitive, xxiv, 46, 51, 70–72; and play, 57–58, 65–68; poetic, xxiv, 31–33, 51, 55, 69–72; public, 30–31; sacred, xiii, 5, 16, 50, 71, 75–77, 88; social, 45; third, xxvin7, 72; and time, 1–5, 16, 42, 52n24, 64, 66; and worship, 4, 32. *See also* land; place

Spirit, Holy: as Poetic, 31–33; as *Spiritus Creator*, 29, 32, 55

Stayer, James M., 35n15

stewardship, 46, 68–69

Streufert, Mary J., 34n6

Taylor, Charles, xxviin32

Taylor, Drew Hayden, 19n61

terra nullius, 53n41

Thompson, Deanna, 34n6

Tice, Terrence, 50

Tillich, Paul, xxviin31, 26

time: as *chronos*, 16, 69; as circular, xv–xvi, xxviin32, 10–11, 49; as *kairos*, 16–17, 69, 71; linear, xvi, xxiii, xxviin32, 10–11; and space, 1–5, 16, 42, 52n24, 64, 66, 68

Tinker, George "Tink," xv, xviii, 4, 21, 23–24, 51n7, 84

transcendentals, xvi–xvii; beauty, 47–50; goodness, xx, 43–47; truth, xx–xxiii, 40–43

Trelstad, Marit, 34n6

Trickster, xxii, 14–15, 19n61, 64

trust, 30–33, 79

Truth and Reconciliation Commission of Canada, xxviiin52

Tweed, Thomas, xxvn3

United Nations Declaration on the Rights of Indigenous Peoples, xxviiin53

universalism, xviii, 18n29, 39

Voss Roberts, Michelle, xxviiin48

Westhelle, Vítor, xvi, 16

Wiebe, Rudy, 9

Wilson, Shawn, xxixn60, 87

Wingren, Gustaf, 25–27

Woodley, Randy, 11–12, 40, 82, 86

World Council of Churches, 77, 85

About the Author

Allen G. Jorgenson is Assistant Dean, Professor of Systematic Theology, and holds the William D. Huras Chair in Ecclesiology and Church History at Martin Luther University College at Wilfrid Laurier University, Waterloo, ON, Canada. He has contributed many book chapters on the topic of comparative theology, with special interest in the question, "What might Christians learn from Indigenous spiritualities and worldviews?" His most recent publication is "Decolonizing and Indigenizing Liberation Theology" in *Post-Christian Interreligious Liberation Theologies*. He is co-editor of *Strangers in this World: Multireligious Reflections on Immigration*. He also publishes in the areas of Martin Luther and Friedrich Schleiermacher. Allen enjoys painting, poetry, and sailing when not immersed in theology.

www.ingramcontent.com/pod-product-compliance
Lightning Source LLC
Chambersburg PA
CBHW050910300426
44111CB00010B/1463